Date Like A Grownup

Names and non-essential physical and biographical details of some of the men and women in this book have been altered to protect privacy. This book is not intended to replace the professional services of licensed psychologists, psychiatrists or social workers. The observations and principles outlined in this book were developed through the author's own experiences as well as from the reported stories of hundreds of men and women navigating midlife dating.

Paperback edition ISBN 978-0-9913493-0-2

Cover photo by Brenda Butler Kerns
Cover design by Laura Stepp
Book design by Unauthorized Media

www.heatherdugan.com
Published by HDC Press 2014

Also by Heather Dugan

Pickup in Aisle Twelve

Stuffing Sandwiches Down My Shirt: Strategies and Inspiration for Crutch Users

Date Like A Grownup:

anecdotes,
admissions of guilt
&
advice between friends

By Heather Dugan

HDC Press, Columbus, Ohio

"Date Like a Grownup: Anecdotes, Admissions of Guilt & Advice Between Friends" examines both the bad and the lucky choices of men and women in their second single lives. Unlike many other relationship manuals, this book will *not* guide you through game playing and winning temporary partners. Instead, readers will develop a personalized strategy for building a life foundation that facilitates growing a "right fit" relationship. Topics include: effective filtering, social media and online dating, how to avoid isolation and strategically building a larger social network. Engaging narratives such as "Parking Lot Apology," "The Percocet Proposal" and "Need Meets Greed" provide the punctuating proof for specific dating principles outlined in the book.

While organized to carry the reader through initial decisions into their practical implementations, feel free to use this book as a reference tool and skip around to your own points of interest. The subtitles are intended to allow the reader easy access to timely information—and, hopefully, inspiration. The "From the Field" anecdotes can be welcome confirmation that we are not alone in making the occasional bad decision, and that we needn't wallow in our failures any longer than necessary to grab our essential lessons and move on to "better."

And with at least half of the adult population attempting a "do-over" on their most committed relationship—and many getting it wrong yet a second time—these proven "do's and don'ts" are first date gold for men and women navigating midlife dating and vicarious entertainment for thankful sideline observers.

Praise for "Pickup in Aisle Twelve"

"Dugan takes you on a heart-felt and often hilarious journey in dating from chance meetings in grocery aisles to online dating disasters and everything in-between. Dugan is charming, witty, and original." —*Nina Munteanu, author of "Darwin's Paradox"*

"Heather Dugan has done an outstanding job of capturing some of the choices, challenges and even occasional humor of life after divorce in the age of digital dating. You will root for Angie to find the right person, and her journey offers fresh insights into the Mars and Venus worlds in which men and women often orbit." —*Dennis Hetzel, author of "Killing the Curse" and Executive Director of the Ohio Newspaper Association*

"Heather Dugan does a great job of being wryly funny, while poking fun of the pitfalls and awkward situations involved in this shark- and quirky guy-infested world of online and blind dating. Her insight expands into family relationships and is quite poignant at times." —*Laura Frongillo; Past editor at Salary.com and Creative Manager at Vista Print*

"Heather Dugan's wit entertains the reader; but in a larger sense her clever humor removes the edge from the sharp, difficult issues Angie must confront in moving forward—making those issues easier to understand and process. 'Pickup in Aisle Twelve': Definitely worth reading! Looking forward to more lessons from Angie Wharton in Profile on Page Nine!" —*Senior HR executive, Fortune 500 company*

Praise for "Stuffing Sandwiches Down My Shirt: Strategies and Inspiration for Crutch Users"

"'Stuffing Sandwiches Down My Shirt...' is a very practical and inspirational look at how to survive and excel in recovering from an injury or in this case, surgery. Ms. Dugan uses her upbeat humor to share her own thoughts and creative solutions to the very real challenges encountered during recovery from surgery." —*Dr. Christopher Hyer; DPM*

"'Sandwiches' is all about attitude with a capital 'A.' This is more than a DIY manual—it's as if Heather becomes your personal mentor urging you to adopt your own 'yes, I can' attitude. We know 'Attitude' affects the healing process —so thank you, Heather, for such an enjoyable and health-enhancing read." —*Monda Sue Prior; MSW, LICSW*

"This book will take you on Heather's journey from the hopelessness of not being able to run again to her spirited triumph over the many obstacles in her way. You will be inspired to put your own 'best foot forward' enthusiastically when faced with challenges." —*Mark Dilworth; BA, PES; Fitness/health author*

"Thank yous" from Salary.com readers

"I have to tell you I enjoy your articles on Salary.com. Being a single dad, I can relate to all your home/work life balance articles and continue to remind myself of many of the things you mention. Thanks for telling it like it is."

"I'm sorry for the TMI message —*laugh*. But you really inspired me! I do like your writing and common sense. So thanks, Heather."

"I loved this advice. My life at 54 with adult daughters living at home has had a big shift since they were little. I am about to go back to full-time at work after a year of part-time, and anxiety is already creeping in. Thanks for the reminders."

"What a terrific article! Even though I recently adjusted my career to stop working 24/7 so that I could be there more for my children, I was (unpleasantly) surprised to find that there still aren't enough hours in the day! Your advice was solid, practical, and much appreciated! And I'm sharing it with my husband!"

Table of Contents

"Loneliness makes fools of us all."

INTRODUCTION

IN MANY WAYS dating as an adult is easier. That whole "who will I be when I grow up" thing is fairly established, and it won't be necessary to endure a semester of algebra with the creep who stood you up for Homecoming. And, best of all, nobody smells like Clearasil.

However…hearts remain fragile, trust is no longer effortless and building any sort of relationship must be done in between parenting and work obligations.

It will challenge you.

Whether you choose to brave an office romance, meet someone over weight sets at the gym or go the online route, you're encountering men who have been shaped by a lifetime of experiences that you weren't a part of. They may be completely out of your social circle, so there's no double-checking amongst your friends. You can Google the hell out of them and check their recommendations on LinkedIn, but none of that will tell you how he treated the last woman he dated, if he calls his mom and if he knows what science class his daughter is taking.

Many of my women friends feel forced to be detectives, sultry sirens and accomplished professionals over a single cup of coffee. Most of the time, the biggest spark comes from the caffeine. Occasionally, however, there's a "click." Maybe…

Will he really call? Will he call in time for us to make plans for the only evening I have free this month?

Fortunately, or unfortunately, there will be more of a paper trail to obsess over this time. Text messages and emails digitally linger for further analysis (or sanity-saving deletion). *What did he mean by, "See ya?"*

And, within your more enclosed worlds at high school or college, there was no "two-timing" without probable discovery. But as a divorced adult, there is a decent chance that one of you flirted with adultery—a whole new level of betrayal. How do you discern and trust against that sort of backdrop?

You're flipping open life stories at the mid-point with no guarantees that you're getting the *full* story.

Sometimes it seems like we're following Edison's tedious methodology of simply eliminating paths to light bulb invention. But knowing what doesn't/didn't/won't work *is* valuable. As a divorced single woman for over eight years now with a network of similarly single male and female friends, I've gathered some practical information from our joint experiences—some solid principles as well as some bendable rules. There are characters and scenarios to avoid and some basic concepts with which you can make better choices. There are ways to open your heart slowly and guard against laying it near some stranger's muddy work boots.

This book contains the collected conversations and cringe-worthy "can't believe I did that" stories of some very accomplished professional women—our cabernet analyses of dating disasters and some pinpoint mapping of the landmines and our own missteps. Pour a glass and join us—or make it a coffee if it isn't five-o-clock in your part of the world. Learn how to navigate the obstacles, avoid repetitive relational roundabouts and roll down your windows for the open road ahead.

Date like a grownup, and build relationships that add value to your life.

CHAPTER ONE

YOU GO FIRST

IN THE BEGINNING there was focused lip-gloss application and excess use of push up bras. Some of my cohorts mixed it up with cooking classes and extra gym workouts. We transitioned from being divorced or single to being "available" and, ostensibly, "relationship ready."

Only many of us weren't. My first random post-divorce dates included a neighbor (bad idea), another neighbor (yet another bad idea) and a property mogul who made the news for a hazmat situation by our third date. My first two choices resulted in some awkward "eyes on the horizon" dog walking—the neighbors lived directly across the street from one another—and the third became an anecdote. My guy friends' first date disasters include pill-popping ladies seeking immediate commitment and the appearance of ex-boyfriends who didn't yet realize that a prefix had been added to their romantic status. Girlfriends dangled their hearts within reach of players already intent on their next roll of the Match.com dice. Clearly, there was more to dating than simply hanging up a shingle and posting an online profile.

These are deep and murky waters. It can be hard to separate the genuine from the well camouflaged, so it's important to at least be clear on the things you can control.

Your Intentions

Are you bored? Lonely? Trying to get even with your ex? Looking for a potential life-mate?

Before you can be honest with others, you need to square up with yourself. Recreational or casual daters are short-term planners, and won't need to be as particular as a relationship-seeker who is searching for someone with whom to share her life. I am assuming that readers of this book are dating with intention and that you, the reader, are looking for a long-term partner and, possibly, marriage.

So first, if you are looking for a life partner, resolve *not* to waste your time going out with someone who is simply unwilling to commit himself to another. This isn't to say that you start off a first date by researching the compatibility of your furniture, but *do* measure your dating decisions against your long-term intention. A guy that isn't headed in the same direction will tear at your heart.

Your Boundaries

Establish the playing field and the rules before you enter the game, or you will run the risk of getting tackled as you're gauging wind direction. What are acceptable locations for "meet-and-greets" with blind dates? Are you willing to risk the potential embarrassments in dating co-workers, fellow school parents or gym members? You won't have mom or dad or friends quizzing you on the "bases" covered in a new relationship—well, your friends might—but you *do* have emotional and mental boundaries on what will feel comfortable to you: Can you identify them? Regrets are ugly and self-defeating. Try to avoid them by being your own parent.

Your Stability

Are you ready for this? Seriously. We're not talking wardrobe and banter here. Are you emotionally stable and healed from the hurts and general weathering you've endured?

For many years, I took pride in my strength, but my wounds ran deeper than divorce and included some childhood traumas. In my late thirties, I bowed under the death of both parents within five months, followed closely by my grandfather's death and my own major surgery. Then came three years of divorce proceedings, more death, more heartbreak and general floundering. *And this is the vastly abridged version...* My feet weren't even aimed at the ground when I first began dating in my early forties. I had confident moments but a long way to go on emotional healing from all of my difficult life events. Two serious relationships tanked when I withdrew. I dated the wrong guys for the wrong reasons. Nothing felt right—but I didn't know what was wrong.

Good solid therapy and treatment for Post Traumatic Stress Disorder (PTSD) made all the difference and gave me much needed perspective. I established essential boundaries and aimed for resilience over simple strength. I pulled myself out of the dysfunctional crowd and stepped over to solid ground.

I'll be honest. This causes problems now. Many of the men that might have felt nurturing to my wobbly self don't fit at all with the stronger me of today. I'm reconciled to the fact that my evolved standards may diminish my available prospects. But you know what? A good life will drive itself. I would rather be alone with me than lonely with the wrong guy. I'm looking for good quality icing. I already have the cake.

So…are you ready? Dating will not fix your mean mother, your cheating ex-spouse, your shaky finances or your dead career dreams. It's only *dating*. Hopefully, one stranger will become your new best friend. But dating is likely to bring repeated miseries unless you can first stand, alone yet complete, with confidence and joy. Relationships won't create a life. They will only, hopefully, enrich the one you have already built.

Also, it's unlikely that you'll meet "the One" or at least "One of the Possible Ones" immediately. Remember interviewing for jobs? Taking college courses toward a degree? Look forward to that sort of marathon experience again as you connect with new people, learn more about yourself within the context of others and search for the "right fit." Your instincts may fail you. A new love may fail you. There is a lot of risk with no guarantees. It can be painful.

Why do people do this??

Oh yeah… Significant connection enhances what we already have and can help us grow into better people. And it's nice to share popcorn with someone on purpose rather than just dropping stray kernels to your hopeful dog.

But connection after divorce has to be bigger than one single romantic relationship. Your social network must grow to where one single person does not have the ability to rock your balance and drain your joy. Young romance luxuriously absorbed almost your complete focus. Later life romance will require compromise, discipline and determination to flourish.

And those rose colored glasses that made your ex look so good are now likely to be bifocals—essential to your multidirectional life. The goal is to find "the one… worth suffering for"[1] without losing the one worth nurturing. Yourself.

From the Field: *"On The Market At The Market"*

In the end, it was my beginning.

While in the midst of a double divorce—my simultaneous extrication from both a nineteen-year marriage as well as the affair that had amplified marital deficits—I hit a Walmart en route to a family dinner.

My flouncy skirt was a significant upgrade from my standard gym-ready shopping attire, and once I identified the tapping sounds penetrating the grocery cart's wheel whine as my own two-inch heels, they gained cadence. I was in my own little parade, feigning straight-backed confidence—but praying I wouldn't topple over while turning my head to read a store sign.

At first, I simply pretended not to notice him.

As I was seeking a recognizable brand of bread with a freshness date that would last beyond the drive home, I caught a flicker of motion to my right. It was a double take. While I've often done the same for domed cheese cubes, we were beyond the range of likely food samples, so I casually glanced to the left, looking for the point of interest.

Empty aisle.

I swiveled slowly to place the winning loaf of whole wheat

into my cart and let my eyes slide up to an exceptionally friendly smile near aisle's end. His face barely registered as I froze, averted my eyes, smiled vaguely at the pita bread and wheeled on toward produce, fairly certain that I'd spill off of my heels onto my butt at any moment.

Replenishing produce had been my main shopping objective, and it took me a few minutes to load up on bananas, tomatoes and all my other essentials. By the time I made the least lengthy checkout line, I'd completely forgotten the smiling stranger in the bread aisle.

"Hi there."

He beamed at me. The bread aisle man.

"Um, hi." I racked my brain to remember which soccer team or classroom or committee I knew him from.

"I couldn't help noticing you have a beautiful smile."

Instant relief. I didn't need to remember his name.

Followed by a flow of dread. *He's trying to pick you up!* The voice was mine, but the tone belonged to my deceased, culturally careful mother.

The whole idea of a grocery store pickup felt slightly sleazy. *Trash pickup. "Pick up your room!" "Can you pick up a case of beer on your way over?"*

Did the fact that a stranger was approaching me mean that I was suddenly irresistible? Or was I now exuding an "I'm eating raisin bran for dinner" look that made me fair game for any man with a dinner invitation?

I wanted to tell him Walmart was just on the way to where I was going that particular night. That, usually, I paid more for subdued ambience and softer lighting. I wanted to be standing there with a boyfriend or husband making jokes about the beef jerky in the checkout aisle, knowing that we'd be brushing teeth side-by-side in the master bath later that night.

"Thanks." I smiled again. Smallish. More of a teensy polite grin, really. And then moments later, I cringed when our extended conversation about absolutely nothing held up the checkout line.

It has to get better than this.

And, oh it did...

Weeks later we met again in the produce section of yet another grocery. He gave me the same beaming smile, and I fled, lobbing polite remarks over my shoulder.

"Maybe," I thought, "it's time to make choices rather than respond to random moments in my life. What are the odds that Mr. Right is going to show up at my gym on the day I remembered to wear a non-compressing sports bra? Maybe this is why people try online dating?"

CHAPTER TWO

ONLINE OR OFF?

ONLINE DATING gets a bad rap—and rightly so, in many cases. I once arranged to bump into a Match.com date at a health food grocery, so that if we liked each other well enough to date, we could just say we met by the bananas.

But if you don't want to date a neighbor, co-worker or fellow soccer parent—despite the obvious carpooling potential—what are your other options? After age 40, our social options diminish a bit, and none of us want to be the female equivalent of the comb-over guy with the heavy cologne and yellowed teeth leering awkwardly from the edge of the dance floor. Yes, there are MeetUp groups, sports clubs and business networking events, but as we age, we also more closely define and inherently limit ourselves. Potential has actualized into some specific choices by midlife. We are becoming, hopefully, our best, most authentic selves.

There is an exfoliation of the extraneous as we become

more focused toward our unique passions and pitfalls. The male personae that attracted you as a younger woman has now been chiseled, or bumped and bruised, into what was probably lurking beneath all along. *Psst... It happened to us too, but we call it "refinement."* The former football star may have channeled his motivation into a business that leaves him with little time for physical fitness. He may be less concerned with saving the world and more focused on saving for his kids' college educations. The future novelist may have landed in IT, and the straight A achiever may have had trouble performing in a dynamic real world environment. These personal evolutions siphon a lot of *former* potential mates right out of the dating pool. Life has chipped away at some of the surfaces of the average post forty-year old man and revealed what was yet to be defined when he was a less formed twenty-something.

The "positive?" Late bloomers are thriving by now, revealing appealing texture that may have been hidden under youthful insecurities. While the selection will be smaller by our forties, it's not so much of a grab bag purchase—you have the option of knowing your partner a lot better, because he is more fully grown towards who he will become. It's no "full" disclosure, but you're seeing the Ferrari after it's weathered a few city miles. The new car smell is gone, but performance is more clearly established.

So, online dating *may* be a good option if you are swimming in a small pool—just don't allow it be your *only* option.

Approach it with oven mitts on both hands.

There are some desperate and damaged people out there, and many of them gravitate to online dating sites where they can shop returnable merchandise to their heart's content. Whole, healthy people post profiles and pictures as well, but the weeding-out process can be disheartening and time consuming.

An air-brushed profile that draws your attention online often turns out to be the "can't return it fast enough" Amazon purchase that arrives on your doorstep looking nothing like the five star product you ordered.

Magic happens, but don't let sideshow trickery distract or divert your focus. This is where your larger network and personal antennae will gain importance. You will need both skeptics and cheerleaders, and you will benefit from the opportunities provided by a large and growing social network.

Online and offline networking will bring you more potential connections. So, spread a wide net. Not to "catch" anyone, but simply to hold your possibilities. There are more than you think.

From the Field: *"Emptied Nest"*

There were tears—garnished with a few expletives and some happy hour-priced wine... A husband of more than twenty years had left, and Nancy was slowly uncovering next step options.

Joining my friends and me was a brave move. Facing an empty house, she had opted for conversation over the hum of a half-filled dishwasher. She ordered the pot stickers and divulged.

"He finally told me on Mother's Day." Stoic smile. "His happiest years were with me, he says—but he's done. Just like that. Twenty years down the drain." She was angry. Puzzled. "I told him he's a complete stranger to me. I don't know him anymore." She shrugged her shoulders to show she didn't care, amplifying how very much she did. "So... here I am: an almost-divorced woman with a big assed empty nest. How do I do this?! I'm not ready to date yet, but it's so damned lonely! How do I meet someone?"

The question was directed to us, but her eyes hopefully scanned a table of suited men at the next table. Wedding rings...I'd already checked.

"I met my husband at work."

"Go online."

She shook her head. "Not ready for that. I just want something casual. Not ready for anything serious."

"When will the divorce be finalized?"

"Filing at the end of the year. I'm kind of in limbo, but he's screwing Mandy. I'll be damned if I sit at home by myself."

"Go online. I'm telling you. It's the quickest way to meet a bunch of eligible men."

In the end, she opted for the combo—putting herself out in the social stream of networking and social events while also posting a bare bones online profile.

She accompanied me to a friend's business kickoff event at a trendy Short North restaurant the following week and clicked with a similarly wronged friend whose new life already had a comfortable, lived-in feel. Carla was Nancy's first post-divorce friend, and rebuilding officially began.

Nancy found familiar faces at our next outing, a charity networking event. It was a friendly group, and she seemed to enjoy herself, even relishing attention from a single man or two. The hardest part seemed to be selecting appropriate sharing levels. There was no easy answer to "How are you?" *Everything* somehow related to the story of how her husband had left her for a co-worker. Her bitterness was understandable, but potentially a dam in her forward surge.

A friend expressed her concerns to me privately. "She's going to burn bridges."

"It's a stage. We just need to help her see the bigger picture. This is the hardest part. She's reinventing. You went through this when you divorced Joe last year."

"Yeah. Finding out who I am without him was hard. Scary. I'm *still* figuring it out. But ultimately *I'm* the only one who can do it."

"Same for Nancy, I think. She's making friends and beginning to take the initiative in planning things. That's really big."

Nancy joined a few of us for a dance night. Dancing was one of the "favorite things" her ex had taken when he left, and Nancy was primed to grind out some cardio.

She had scabbed knees from her new boot camp addiction, sculpted arms and curves in all the right places. She lubricated herself to hit the dance floor with pumpkin ale and got down to business flirting with some Aussies in town for The President's Cup Golf Tournament before moving on to the twenty-ish hip hop band members.

"Who needs him!" She laughed over her shoulder to me. Tonight she didn't, and I was glad, gamely fighting my maternal urge to tie a tether on her. It was a beginning. And that was all she needed to grow a little hope and begin to take action.

Presently, she's seeing some Italian she met online, has regained a sex life and basically disappeared. Temporarily. Rarely is the first guy the "right guy." I'm hoping for the best, but at least she now has a group of women friends to lean on if he isn't.

Chapter Three

Choosing Your Filters

HE APPROACHED ME at the checkout lane; handed over his card and suggested coffee. Prior to that special Walmart moment, it hadn't really occurred to me that I was "dateable." For the first few months after my divorce I'd been gunning to make Super Mom, re-launching my earlier career and figuring out how to change the oil in my lawn mower. All of a sudden, I was a woman again. My ringless left hand, reaching for the cash register receipt, looked naked. Exposed. Thereafter, I alternated between stuffing my left hand into a pants pocket and casually swirling it through my hair, making sure my ring finger didn't disappear beneath a curl. Complicated? No kidding!

Dating is a *lot* more complex by mid-life. And it isn't always clear if we—or the seemingly available men—are actually out in the field or on an extended bench break.

During our early dating years, everyone had pretty much traveled the same route. Awkward moments and unwise choices were mutually recognized and acknowledged. It was likely that life experiences would align more closely because there had been less variant paths available.

By mid-life, however, there has been opportunity for a wealth of adventures well beyond the range of a younger man or woman. That nice guy from the gym who invited you out for a drink could be exactly as he seems—dedicated, energized and blessed with a high performance cardio capacity.

Or not. He may have had three wives because he can't quite commit to one woman or may never have married because he is over-committed to a career. He may feel driven to compensate for a missed youth—or selfish because he's been catered to and unnecessarily accommodated. You may overhear a thing or two in the locker room or at the water-cooler, but primarily, this will be *your* investigation.

Instead of simply searching for the right "click," you will also have to do some filtering. "Mr. Right" may actually be "Mr. Could-Have-Been-Right." Timing, mismatched life experiences and your levels of resiliency may shift a sure thing to a complete mistake.

The First Round Filters

Comparing Intentions

On an online dating site like Match.com, OKCupid, Zoosk or Plenty of Fish (POF), relationship goals can be clearly stated: "Long-term," "casual dating," "marriage"… This doesn't mean that words typed onto a profile will match actual intentions, however. Remember that a profile is often whom a person wants to be. In actuality, he may be a few yards short of the finish line. However, there are clues. *"Just checking this out…"* means exactly what it sounds like. This guy is testing the waters and seeing what he lands on his fishing line. *"Looking for fun-lovin' woman"* again states a clear intention. *"Fun-lovin'"* would be the woman who wants to "play" without any sort of commitment. This virtually guarantees that *"fun-lovin'"* guy will attract *"effed-up"* woman—don't inadvertently put yourself on that list!

If you're looking to build a committed relationship, don't get distracted by an attractive package. That gift-wrap is going to come off, and it's disposable.

Compatible Values

No, you can't mine the depths of his value system over a quick chat at the bookstore or from an online profile, but you can at least note obvious departure points. For instance, if the bookstore guy starts namedropping local celebrities or if the dating site photos are primarily of the guy's expensive vehicles—this is a message. Read it. Accoutrements will be a draw for some women, and that's fine—*There's truly someone for everyone*—but that focus would not match my top tier values and I would quickly move on. Not because he exhibits signs of financial or social success—*Horrors!*—but because anyone who believes those to be his best asset is going to be lacking some of the other, more important, qualities I'm looking for.

So, define what is undeniably essential to you. How will you feel about a guy who is an absentee father—or a guy who prefers lifting pints to free weights? There are no "right" answers, but there are "right fits." Dating as a grownup is hard enough. Avoid making successful connection even more difficult. Don't compromise on ideals that will create drag when reality kicks in.

Key values to consider include: family connectivity, health/

fitness (emotional and physical), importance of friendships (or is he a loner?) and his spiritual beliefs.

Congruent Philosophies

These may be political, socioeconomic or spiritual. Their weight on a relationship will depend upon level of passion and degree of commitment. Sure Democrats and Republicans can mix, but a die-hard Democrat and uber-conservative activist is an unlikely pairing. Similarly a "succeed at all costs" type of personality is unlikely to resound well with a compassionate service-oriented individual no matter how combustible the chemistry. Hunters and vegans? Spendthrifts and the financially frugal? Respect is critical to relationship success, and if you despise a guy's approach to life, it won't matter how perfect everything else looks on paper. The same goes for all things spiritual. An atheist and a fundamentalist Christian might generate some sparks, but how will they navigate Sunday mornings?

One big consideration will be the degree to which your underlying motivational currents are in sync. A "happiness-seeker" won't fit well with an individual focused on mining for "meaning" in his or her life. Chemistry may be enough congruence for some men, so be prepared to make a solo decision on this.

Geographical Challenges

Have love; will travel? Some do, but it's hard. I know friends who won't consider the other side of town much less another city as well as people who are willing to commute state-to-state for the right partner.

I would suggest that while long-distance might (have to) work for an already existing relationship, building an authentic connection from afar is exceptionally difficult. A geographically challenged relationship can be a fairytale escape for those not quite ready for commitment or one long heartache for those who are.

Getting to know someone requires hanging out together in ordinary moments and surviving a few crises together. You'll never know how he handles an overflowed toilet if the two of you are on a "meet halfway in Chicago once a month" sort of schedule. Don't you think it's important to know those kinds of things? I do. Traveling with someone will reveal how they treat strangers and handle mishaps and uncertainty. But I also want to know how a guy chooses between TV football and a beautiful outdoor day and what he does when the seafood counter has inferior salmon.

Part-time "perfect" is easier to find than full-time "real."

Educational Differences

Differing education levels can be problematic or no problem at all. Ultimately a college degree is no measure of an individual's ability to learn throughout his or her lifetime, but a degree can indicate discipline and the value placed on personal growth. On the other hand, a guy with an undergraduate degree who views books as paperweights and "news" as headlines to be gleaned in the supermarket checkout lane probably won't be conversational on world events.

Typically, a similar educational background is one more weight in a relationship's favor, but this is for you to decide. A college-educated man could still be highly ungrammatical— and some of us are sticklers on spelling and sentence structure. A "life" educated man may turn out to be the more fascinating conversationalist. Alas, neither of the aforementioned educations is a guarantee that he has learned to properly adjust a toilet seat.

The most important thing will be if *his* brain and *your* brain connect.

Age Ranges

Many men will only date younger women. *All together now: "Their loss!"* Some women similarly limit themselves by narrowly defining their own "dateable" age group. For a long time I did this myself, refusing to date anyone more than two years older or younger than me. While that might have made sense during college, I eventually found my random age limitation to be an antiquated notion—because when I analyzed the "why" behind that inclination, I found it was actually tied to my preconceptions on life experience.

As a college senior, I briefly dated a man in his mid-twenties. While he was only three years older, we lived in vastly different worlds. I still don't know what he, a young account executive, found so fascinating about a sorority girl cramming in classes for a hastily added business minor. *Well, besides my obvious ability to recite the Greek alphabet, I guess.* It was soon apparent—to me at least—that we had little to talk about.

Similarly, after enduring a few family and personal tragedies, I found it difficult to relate in a meaningful way with men who hadn't yet been at least slightly challenged by life. But this was not age-related—it was instead, a measure of how these men had explored and experienced life by the time we met.

Viewing a man as the sum of his life experiences rather than as a biological age will better facilitate finding a real and lasting connection. While it's wise to have a general age range in mind, don't narrow your funnel unnecessarily. Maturity is never tied to age. Look at activity level, sense of adventure and life experience to get the full picture of how old a man truly is. Some men never grow up. Others simply never grow.

Gauging Attraction

This was much simpler before our brains and bellies grew. He flashed a smile over the shoulder of his letter jacket, and you inked his name inside a heart on a bathroom stall door.

By our forties physical attraction is threaded with memories and history. If he shares your ex's crooked smile, you may not be inclined to share your heart. Time has passed and done an acid etch on some of us, revealing underlying attitudes and the weathering effects of our chosen life paths.

Many of my friends experience instant "2D" attractions to an online photo or a weight bench buddy. For some of us, however, attraction will spark or fizzle only over the course of conversation, when an attractive or nondescript appearance gains 3D texture with verbal connection, physical demeanor and eye contact. Those who experience 2D attraction may open a wider range of initial possibilities. These friends tend to dive into relationships quickly with varying results. With those for whom physical chemistry is hardwired to an intellectual connection, it may often seem there are no possibilities in sight. These people may do better developing friendships and simply waiting to see if time and texturing create attraction that could lead to a dating relationship.

Be real with yourself. A few solitary Saturdays can lead some of us toward the least negative option on our missed call list, which is never a good idea.

If you think that you *might* want to kiss him in *dim* lighting after a *couple* glasses of cabernet? Move on. Can you really imagine a *forever* that necessitates chugging wine and unscrewing light bulbs? Or maybe you prefer him to smile silently—because he ruins the attraction factor every time he opens his mouth to speak... Don't waste your time and his heart. Feeling alone with the wrong guy is a lot worse than having a little extra closet organization time. Make your life bigger than dinner and a movie.

To Google or Not to Google?

Electronic ogling provides an excellent extra layer of safety to meeting a dating site contact. And, a digital search has yanked willing hearts back from possible breakage when a new man's story didn't quite match up with his actions. However, Googling can also remove the enticing sense of mystery and create disengaging preconceptions about a new dating connection.

Truthfully, the online dating era probably prevents as many potentially good relationships as it initiates. We become back room decision-makers, selecting and deselecting people we've never met based on minutia, which plays nicely into the whole Attention Deficit Disorder (ADD) approach that online dating fosters.

So, Google lightly. He should at least show up on LinkedIn, allowing you to confirm that he is indeed gainfully employed in his stated city of residence. Facebook? TMI, in my opinion. Resist the temptation to study up on a date or meet-and-greet. Let *him* tell you how much he enjoys cycling or that his son is a star soccer player over that first cup of coffee. Try to save the detective work for your face-to-face when you can both ask and respond to some general "get to know you" questions.

Similarly, remember that you, also, are a Google search

term. Revealing your last name is keycard access to your online history. Your websites, links, connections and affiliations—even your property ownership—are unlocked for perusal and judgment. He may not be search savvy or even curious, but be aware of what an Internet search will reveal. Social media opens up new connections but can also provide a flood of information that can affect the current of a new dating relationship. Pace the flow of personal information.

Further Refinements

You kissed him and are on your way to a third date. After you've shared your best stories, figured out whom you know in common and that you were at the same Eric Clapton concert, it's time to evaluate deeper currents. That first rush is thrilling, but it's a "spark," not a campfire. Focused anticipation—when you shift from hoping to meet *someone* to hoping to see someone in particular—is the heart-fluttering, silly smile, sing-aloud in the car stuff that zips you right back to your memories of those earlier dating years. It's fun! You begin building a mental catalogue of glances, touches and spoken phrases to flip through in idle dreamy moments. If you've been single very long, the very idea that someone "likes you," can make you like *him* a **lot**. This is where dating like a grownup will necessarily deviate from dating like your younger self.

There's more at stake now and less time lying ahead of you. *Sorry!* If you're able to step aside for a moment and evaluate the following with a close and stable friend or therapist, it's in your best interest to do so.

Complementary Lifestyles

In the beginning, there may be some magical mirroring. *"He loves to do all the same things!"* OK, maybe he actually enjoys antiquing, but since when were you into ice hockey? He may express interest in yoga, art and reading your book club selection, but when the water settles, his interest may land at a lower level.

The thing is, when something interesting crosses our path, we have a tendency to accelerate.

Picture yourself pedaling your bike along a trail on a sunny day. Suddenly, you spot an attractive man merging ahead of you. He's no stranger to a bike saddle. And those arms… *Bet he pumps some iron too.* His profile passes muster as he turns onto the trail under a shimmer of sunlight, so you shift gears and pedal just a little faster. *It was time to ramp it up a little anyways. You were practically coasting those last two miles!* He's flying though, so you have to work a little. At some point you admit that you're lamely trying to chase him down, and he's making you work for it. Finally, he glides to the side and reaches down for his water bottle. *OK. A real cyclist would have kept pedaling. But maybe he noticed you too? Maybe he has pulled aside to see if you're worth a smile.* You glide up and sure enough, he glances up and grins. Turns out he's not your type. Something about his smile reminds you of an uncle you never warmed up to. You nod quickly and pedal on.

My point? We are capable of performance when it comes to engaging with a target. It won't always be genuine, however. Your 20 mph sprint faded to a more modest pace as you pedaled on past your Uncle Andy's twin. Similarly, a guy's newly discovered fascination with yoga may die once he's assured you'll be available on his free weekends.

How to navigate? Discover common interests but also

delve into history. A guy who's excited to get back into the gym is not as invested in his health as the guy who is already working out five times a week. A man who wants to travel but has no passport is not as curious about the world as the one who soloed to Spain last summer. Yes, we grow and learn from one another, and dating your twin self sounds kind of creepy, but it's remarkably easier if you share some primary passions and are already traveling in the same general direction.

Maturity Issues

It wasn't a long conversation, but it revealed a lot. My friend Charlene and I were nailing down details for a double date, having discovered that the men we were dating knew one another from criss-crossing paths through the tangled political and economic evolutions of our state. They'd never played on the same team but respected one another's abilities and integrity. Charlene and I deemed this worthy of a dinner date.

Charlene had already met the guy I was bringing to the table and given full approval. "John's pretty hot. I see why you like him."

"Yeah! He's really smart, and that is so sexy to me. And there's the handsome face and fitness thing too. To be totally shallow…"

We laughed, and then I asked. "So what's the hesitation with Gary?"

"Well… He's had a couple of DUIs. He was very upfront about that, and we talked about the circumstances. I understand how both happened…" Her voice trailed off. I waited.

"But, well he called kind of last minute one night to see if I'd go out, and I'd already made plans, so I said 'no thanks,' because I am not going to chart my life around whether I get a phone call from a guy!" *One reason I like Charlene so much is that she likes herself enough to "walk the walk."* "So, he says, 'Guess I'll just go get drunk then. Haha…' I thought he was joking! But I'm out with my girlfriends later that night, and I start getting all these drunk texts and then, finally a phone call—slurred speech, the whole deal—and I thought, how *old* is this guy?"

Here's the thing. We're supposed to learn from our bad choices and youthful indiscretions and switch out those mistakes for age appropriate/socially responsible behavior. Once parenthood hits, frat kegger shenanigans are typically relegated to party stories—pulled out when there's nothing better to talk about. It's "been there, done that" stuff that doesn't bear repeating.

Loser behavior can manifest in many ways besides the obviously unsafe and/or illegal. Is he stuck in time or attempting some ill-advised time travel? I once dated a guy who wanted to hang out in bars with twenty-year olds. He was in his late thirties, and I was over forty and didn't much care to bump into my college age son on a dance floor sticky with spilled beer. My date was still chasing "the cool kids," not realizing that the more engaging personalities of our generation had moved on to more age appropriate venues.

Other "loser behaviors" include anger issues, such as always having to win the freeway merge or being the guy most likely to throw a beer bottle at a TV football fumble, prejudice against other races/nationalities, genders, religions or sexual orientations, and a lazy "last spoon in the sink cleans the dishes" attitude.

Not to be judgmental, but "loser behaviors" are often a maturity issue. You need to date a grownup.

Financial Compatibility

Ok. This is a delicate area. *It's about your bank accounts.* Simply put, it will be easier if the zeros more or less line up. Not to put a price tag on true love, but if he's scrimping to pay his cable bill and you're a pedicure-a-week kind of gal, it could get awkward when you get around to discussing vacation plans. Yes, "love (sometimes) conquers all." But who wants to "conquer?" Wouldn't you rather blend a little? "Conquering" isn't always a "win."

Some work around this. One of my more successful friends actually hides her house. Yeah, any guy worth his Googling salt could eyeball property values via the county auditor site, but Amy downplays her considerable achievements, knowing that they might intimidate—or attract—some men. She doesn't allow dates to pick her up at home until she feels relatively secure of his intentions. For her, it's unlikely that any man will match her "zeros." So she, instead, conceals the bit about her crazy success for a while in hopes of finding a financially stable and emotionally secure man who won't be swayed one way or the other by her degree of achievement—or her loveable pit-bull Annie.

Divorce rarely produces a positive financial impact. Child support, spousal support, giving up the economies of couplehood and setting up a separate household...these can burden a divorced man for many years. So look for A) stability—if he's tapped out his 401K to pay two mortgages, be wary, and B) financial philosophy—is he a spender, saver or something in between, and will this match with your approach?

Do NOT jeopardize your hard-earned financial stability with a financially incompatible man. And, if you're still finding your post-divorce sea legs monetarily-speaking, make it a priority to grow and maintain your financial independence. Do NOT allow money to improve a man's character or attractiveness. Being financially strong will always allow you to make better dating and long-term relationship decisions.

I still shake my head at an old boyfriend who loaned a woman mortgage money during their short three-month relationship. She was still paying it off while he and I dated. Awkward.

Commitment to Communication

My ex-husband and I had our first disagreement in a department store china department.

"These are kind of nice." I twirled a casually elegant wine glass in his direction.

He frowned. "I don't know."

"Maybe these?" I nodded toward another set of sparkling glasses.

He grunted and turned away, eyeing the exit.

There was a sudden frosty silence as we stiffly surveyed the remaining crystal. Internally, my mind screamed, "OMG! Am I marrying the wrong man?"

Yeah. Really. It's kind of embarrassing to recall that pivotal moment in housewares, but a stemware conflict made me question the strength and depth of our love, because, at that point in my life, I envisioned "true love" as a cloning. While I didn't want my future husband to physically look like me—*just at me, adoringly*—I expected him to essentially be "Heather" on the inside.

Love meant agreement. Our brains would jump to the same starry-eyed conclusions. He wouldn't hurt me because I'd constantly be on his mind, and he'd instinctively know the path to making Heather feel good about herself and our relationship. What would we ever have to argue about?

While that sounds obviously naïve and self-centered, I'm surprised how often I hear women say, "He should just *know* that I need/hate/want/hope…!" Somehow, many of us seem to believe that love will open up a mental pipeline to facilitate 24/7 mindreading.

Rather than broaching a relational "disconnect" with a steady hand, we toss out a loaded clue to our unengaged partner, hoping it will land directly on the reverse switch in his brain.

"Umm, you're watching football with the guys? Well sure, I guess I can just clean the basement or something." A significant silence follows as you wait to see if your masked signal has been detected…

The hinting method is haphazard and frustrating to both the crumb-thrower and the intended receiver.

Flash-forward to Post-Divorce Boyfriend Number One after an upstairs shower leak in my home led to a lower level laundry room renovation.

"And see how this just sucks it all up?" He was enthusiastically siphoning dog hair from a crevice in the woodwork with the nozzle on my vacuum cleaner. "Isn't this great??"

"Umm…yeah." My mind wandered to my mom, telling ten-year old me how much fun it would be to clean the garage. I mustered a smile and wondered how soon I'd be able to launder the kids' soccer uniforms again.

Boyfriend Number One was sending me a message— about my dog Lily and her seasonal shedding—but I missed it. I also missed the signal that his feelings were hurt when I broke a date later that week to finish some website work.

"It's fine!"

His higher-pitched voice didn't sound especially happy, but I heard "fine" and rolled with that until our relationship also rolled on to its conclusion shortly thereafter. Ironically, we engaged in our most honest conversations during the breakup and its aftermath.

To be fair, I had my own difficulties in making clear "this sucks" statements. In fact, my common reaction to a significant other missing obvious clues on what Heather really thought, wanted or feared was to freeze like a deer caught in the halogens. Fear sent any appropriate words spinning into orbit where I could no longer string them together. Any perceived or imagined affront rendered me rigid, knees tucked to my face in a vain attempt to disappear, silently waiting for my partner to come up with the right words to release me again. No one ever knew the magical words. But, how could they? I didn't even know how to spell them.

So let's do the math here… One non-communicator with another non-communicator isn't going to add up to open communication, and a communicator paired with a non-communicator is going to get pretty frustrated, right?

So, it's going to take two verbally capable adults to maintain a strong long-term connection. Two committed communicators. Because the unimportant things of life will occasionally get in the way—they always do. Family challenges, overloaded schedules, work commitments… They'll always be there. But will he?

You can spend three years trying to draw him out of his shell, or you can acknowledge that he might be happier snuggled in there with his remote and ESPN—and free yourself to new possibilities.

Be ready to talk. Be ready to listen and connect. The so-called "strong silent type" is often a weak and intimacy-averse companion. Aim higher. For him and for yourself.

Parenting Priorities

Phantom fathers give me pause. They never see their children because of distance or unfavorable custody arrangements. Sometimes these situations are truly beyond their control and will change with time. In other instances, a guy has simply given up or wasn't emotionally attached to his children in the first place.

This is critical information because it can reveal his values, his ability to connect and his strength of spirit.

Single parents are parents first and "single" second.

One of Danielle's guys had children living on the west coast and a grandchild he had never met. I had "passed" on this Match.com guy when our meet-and-greet revealed his three divorces, but "Danielle" was attracted to his rugged vulnerability and deemed the situations to be beyond his control. In time, it became sadly apparent that childhood sexual abuse had left this man unable to form lasting relationships. His desire to connect was genuine, but his ability to do so had been sadly disabled.

Alternately, I dated a guy whose children ran the show. Watching him cower under their judgment and cave in to their Lego demands exposed an unhealthy "need to please" over being an effective and consistent parent. His commitment to his kids was strong and laudable, but the commitment seemed more tied to their approval than his role as their father.

Worst of all are the defeated dads. *"It's no use. I can't fight her attorney." "She (the ex-wife) just won't listen."* If these dads care but lack the emotional strength to effectively deal with their situation, they may spiral into guilt, anger and depression, potentially sucking you toward a precarious perch from which to watch in helpless sympathy.

Now, there *are* extreme situations where parental love may require painful sacrifice and a temporary loss of relationship—kids' needs *always* trump parental wants, and it's better that a parent's heart break than his child's. So, examine intentions to truly understand the choices that led to any rift. Who was he *then*, but more importantly, who is he *now*?

We divorce spouses, but never our children. Unless a man cares enough to consistently strive for some sort of relationship with estranged children via regular attempts at healthy bridge building, his values differ too dramatically from my own for me to consider a long-term relationship with him.

Swivel-Heading

If you've ever dated a guy with this tendency, you already have an image or memory in your mind. Maybe you were sipping wine in a restaurant, discussing which bike trail to cycle on Saturday, and the waitress walked by. His head automatically swiveled away from your conversation and then right back. Your water glasses were recently filled, and you weren't ready for the dinner check. His radar had simply registered "female."

If a guy head-swings on me, I lose interest fast. This can be an indiscriminate habit, but it's disrespectful to all involved.

My ex-husband almost lost me before our marriage by swivel-heading jogging women. When I finally worked up the nerve to mention that it bothered me, he explained that—as a runner himself—he had a habit of noting the form and speed of fellow runners. I said that he seemed to monitor women runners more closely than men. He made a point of practicing gender neutral swiveling for a while until the habit eventually died.

Self-Absorption

If it becomes obvious that he introduced you to the most fascinating person he knows at that initial meet-and-greet, back away. These guys often look terrific because of all the time they spend chiseling their physiques at the gym. But he isn't necessarily looking for a partner so much as a mirror that will provide a great reflection of his favorite person.

This guy tends to instinctively glance toward hallway mirrors—not to catch sight of the two of you together, but to give himself a quick reassuring smile—*Looking good!* Your contributions to conversations will be met with, "That's great. Reminds me of that time I..." He might be good for a few laughs, but once he's shared them all, he'll cue right back up to the beginning and that great story about the time you crawled between skyboxes in a hockey arena to retrieve a free t-shirt will be totally wasted.

Planning Ahead

Guard against simply feeling ignored. "*He's out with clients again tonight...*" It's always best to run these feelings by a trusted friend as some of us tend toward hypersensitivity. But if after a few dates, you consistently remain an afterthought? This relationship isn't headed in a direction you want to go.

Our schedules can be very hard to manage and last minute situations will arise from time to time necessitating our flexibility, but knowing this should spur a new couple to plan ahead. If he isn't making plans with you? He isn't all that interested, and you will be better off either telling him to contact you when his life slows down to a more manageable level or that the relationship simply isn't working for you. Allowing this to continue will drain your self-respect. No guy is worth that kind of trade.

Friend Feedback

"Are you even wearing a push-up bra?"

"Umm... I think so." Quick southward peek. "Well, maybe not."

"Go put on a push-up, get some cleavage and try again!"

That's honest. And that's what I need. I had texted an awkward phone photo to my friend Danielle. She loved the dress, but pushed me (up!) a little. Just as she had when I first started dating. "Eyeliner. Nails. You've got to do the work, girl!"

I thought she was a bit obsessive and probably stomped all the way to my lingerie drawer, to be honest. But I knew she cared about me, so I tried to listen.

Just as I *tried* to take care of her...

"Sign it."

Danielle had sighed and reluctantly reached for the pen. My words had been scribbled out with the inspiration and conviction born of soggy tissues and a bottle of Pinot Grigio. We'd sipped. She'd cried and talked and cried some more. I batted down her excuses and poured her more wine. We edged toward her personal resolution to respect herself.

At which point I'd grabbed a sheet of notepaper to write her a hall pass. "*I promise to never ever ever have contact with Randy because I value myself and choose to be with people who love and respect me as I deserve.*" There was a little Grigio drip toward the end and then her signature, the date and my signed witness.

OK. So she ended up marrying the guy, but the safety net was technically there had Danielle chosen to lean into it. *And I wasn't alone in the puzzled headshaking, by the way. Other friends bet—not on if the marriage would last—but rather on whether it would stretch an entire year! Sadly, it didn't...*

We knew. We tried to tell her. Just as friends have attempted to guide me...

"Umm, you're OK with that?"

"Sure. He's just a little insecure at the moment. He won't do this forever... Will he?"

Our friends know us. They often know what we need. They generally recognize harmful behaviors and situations. Collectively, they are our barometer of how we're handling the pressures in our life.

We need to listen.

Have they met him? Have they spent enough time with him to know a couple of inside jokes? Or is he more of a conversational topic than a guy they'd actually have a conversation with?

Why do we do this? If the boyfriend doesn't fit the life she's built, many a woman will quietly disappear, cupping a hand around the mere spark of a potential relationship and fanning its meager flame in hopes that it will eventually burst into something her friends will gather around. If friends and family matter to you, their opinions are worth your consideration.

Good friends are a valuable resource. They make clear observations and ask valid questions: *"You're not into him"* or *"He's really into his workout routine, isn't he?"* or *"Does he ever take you out to dinner, or do you cook for him every single time?"* If you aren't able to effect a blending of your life BB (Before the new Boyfriend) and AB (After the new Boyfriend), there's something wrong with one of those lives.

From the Field: *"Mixed Up Doubles"*

Few of us possess perfect instincts when it comes to adult dating. It's new. We may feel completely out of our element.

"He seemed normal—maybe a little odd, but I'm an electrical engineer and a bit of a bookworm. A little social awkwardness made him feel more compatible to me."

Carol had met Danny at a community fundraiser. "A friend talked me into going. It was a tennis tournament, and I didn't even know how to hold a racket. But she said, 'That's not the point. It's a fundraiser. We'll give you a racket. Everyone will be nice.'

"So I went and got matched up with Danny. Mixed doubles. I felt like an idiot holding the racket, but he was kind. Made me feel a part of things. We kind of hit it off and met for a drink later that week.

"I met him for dinner the next time and then finally let him pick me up from home for a group thing downtown. At that point, we were dating and continued to see each other for about three months."

She paused. "This isn't funny. It's really kind of creepy."

"So, what happened?"

"Well, I started losing earrings. We were making out on his couch, and I guess that happens… So, I'd ask, 'Did you happen to find an earring?' It happened twice, and each time he said 'Yes, I'll bring it on our next date.'

"But time passed, and when I lost a third earring, I finally called him and asked if I could swing by to pick them up on my way to the gym.

"He met me at the door and invited me in. He didn't have

them in his hand or anything, so I followed him and waited in the family room. He went into his bedroom and then called to me.

"He'd pulled a box from his nightstand, and it was full of earrings. Danny picked them up one by one. 'Not this one. Or this one. Or this one. Or that one…' My stomach dropped. He finally found *my* earrings after laying out a bunch of others on the nightstand. 'Here you go.'

"I don't remember what I said. I just took my earrings and left. I was hurt. Shocked. I had thought we were headed in the right direction and was kind of devastated. Scared."

"Bad dates happen to all of us, but that sounds worse," I agreed.

"I finally worked up the nerve to call him about a week later to kind of ask him about it. He said he was being 'funny.'

"It felt more creepy than funny to me."

I thanked her for sharing the story and invited her to join us for Wednesday happy hour. "It's just a good way to connect with other single women," I told her. "There are a lot of us, and we can help each other."

"I'd like that."

CHAPTER FOUR

POSTING A PROFILE

THE INS, OUTS AND ASIDES of online dating could fill another book. I've personally tried Match.com, Plenty of Fish and eHarmony. Online dating is not for the timid. Without a healthy self-esteem, you run the risk of being sucked into a time-wasting bad relationship. If you have an honest understanding of who you are, however, you won't be so easily swayed or manipulated by the attitudes and opinions of others—and it may give you access to that right guy (who unfortunately has been shopping at the wrong grocery).

The Basics

If you haven't dated in many years and have no idea how to "be available," posting a profile may give you a moderate ego boost and get you off the starting block.

If you post a halfway decent profile, men will be interested. If you are a female who appears to be breathing, men will be interested. In the beginning, it can be an energizing shot in the arm, reminding you that your social life can and will be bigger than a quarterly school conference and ten weeks of middle school soccer.

Conversely, the kinds of men you attract may not be the kinds of men you're looking for.

On many of the most popular sites, *you* are the screener. You will be filtering through a few men whose sincere interest will not flatter you in the slightest and may even alarm you if you're averse to clichés and creative spelling.

What you see will often be more than you want but not nearly enough.

Some misguided souls post bathroom mirror photos, and many of these pictures will be bare-chested attempts to impress females with the six-pack they used to have in high school. Also, what you read will often be highly-euphemized or suspiciously spotty as in: Education: "*I'll tell you later,*" Marital Status: "*I'll tell you later,*" Hobbies/Interests: "*I'll tell you later.*"

It's a dangerous place for the gullible and the wounded.

Don't attempt online dating without some good girlfriend backup. Your discernment skills will be tested, and it's unlikely that your filter will work correctly every time. If you're hurt, lonely or needy—online dating won't make you feel better, it will only keep you very busy.

It's a lot of work.

If you aim to date like a grownup, you'll need to respond to those emails, even if it's a quick copy/paste maneuver. Yep, that means even the sad lonely hearts who aren't anywhere close to "your type." Have I answered every email each time I posted a profile? I sure tried. It can be time consuming, but you aren't allowed to complain about someone ignoring you, if you don't act respectfully toward others.

Thanks for the nice words. Now I do think more highly of you. Not that it might matter, but it leaves a better taste in my mouth about even saying "hi" to someone. —Plenty of Fish response.

You will get "thank yous" for saying "no thank you," and it will help you learn to be a better "kind yet direct" communicator.

Your Profile

This is your dating "resume." While you won't have to list your past experience and explain why you left your last position, you *will* be highlighting your present "qualifications." Your profile is basically a marketing tool, and *you* are the product—so don't sell yourself short. Fill in at least the basic information including a short paragraph about yourself and what sort of relationship and person you are seeking. Share your financial info? Nah. Your favorite *everything*? Nope. Raise a reader's curiosity but don't reveal all of the answers to who you are yet as that may overwhelm—and limit your appeal to a very specific subset of skiing, poetry reading, gluten-intolerant salsa dancers.

Not sure what to say? Ask your friends and family how they would describe you. Even better, grab a girlfriend, a laptop and do a happy hour in your own kitchen. I've helped friends create some authentic and intriguing profiles in this manner over cheese, crackers and cabernet.

Choose a simple sort of mission statement. Avoid dramatic headlines such as "I want to get married this year!" *Commitment-phobes and emotionally healthy men making a stampede exit would slam into the needy and manipulative men honing in on their favorite GPS signal!* Instead, try something like "Seeking another outdoor enthusiast to share my trail mix with" or "Hoping to find a fellow explorer for potential life-long journey."

Be Honest

Being honest means that even though you look amazing in that photo from New Year's Eve, you won't use it if the New Year isn't the current year. Old photos aren't fair. Keep them within six months. Write a comment that includes the actual year if you opt to post an older photo—and there had better be a good reason, such as it features a favorite trip or activity, to land on your profile page.

Don't lie about your age. Men have excused such false information with, "When people meet me, they think I'm a lot younger." My unspoken thought? "Well…same here! So even if you look five years younger, that still puts fifteen years between us!" I remember one man who had gone this route but thankfully had the courage to confess before we met. He was embarrassed when he phoned, but I thanked him and wished him well. It happens frequently enough to be an online dating cliché, but a dishonest start won't take you past a very disappointing cup of coffee.

Don't lie about anything—it's a foundational breach of trust. If a relationship launches from a falsehood, you risk losing it on that inevitable day you finally have to explain there were actually two daddies and three divorces.

It's so nice to finally see a lady who marks her "body type" as "athletic / toned" and who actually IS athletic and toned! Sometimes you look at the people who categorize themselves that way and think, "What are you an athlete at? Pie eating?"

—Match.com response

Be Positive

Being positive will broaden your selection of interested men. Many wounded souls will be excruciatingly honest: *"I'm tired of the games and being used," "Are there any honest guys out there?"* or *"After twenty years in a loveless marriage, it's finally my turn."*

That much detail is overkill and exceptionally negative. No well-intentioned man will be drawn to a negative woman. A manipulative man might, but never the kind of guy you ultimately want to find. Instead of lamenting your divorce, focus on the fresh opportunities ahead of you. Rather than talking about how you don't want to be hurt—*Who does?*—write that you're looking forward to growing something good with the right guy.

Rule of thumb: Say what you want, not what you don't want.

Be Self-Respectful

Being self-respectful means keeping it classy. Men have told me, repeatedly, that obvious cleavage shots and overtly suggestive language are turn-offs. There are no doubt a few men that will pursue a virtual sex ad such as that, but do you really want to explain at the end of the night that you don't consider dinner to be a form of payment? Instead, be friendly, kind and witty. Be YOU. Let him discover your womanly curves when you meet face-to-face—*after* you've ascertained that there is some interest in your brain as well. Similarly, my guy friends comment negatively on multiple partying photos. You can show you're "fun" without repeatedly toasting the camera.

Be Creative

Standing out from the crowd will take a little thought. Look at other women's profiles, but do this with the idea of differentiating—not imitating. You are your own brand. This is cool! If you can *identify* your brand, it will be much easier to promote it authentically.

Are you a great cook? Lovely—*and I'm officially jealous.* But don't say, "I'm a great cook." *Yawn.* Appeal to more than one appetite at a time—"I love making magic happen in the kitchen" or "My kitchen is the Friday night hangout for all of my friends…" Much more interesting.

Are you athletic? A traveler? "Gym bag is always in my trunk," "I pay more attention to my bike tires than the ones on my car," "Would never let my passport expire" or "Prefer back roads to freeways." See what I mean?

Be a Super Bowl ad, not one of those boring "flip past me" jingles you know by heart.

One cautionary note: Being a terrific mom is intrinsic to many of us, but don't make that a focal point of your profile. If a guy reads, "My kids are my life," he will likely think, "sounds like a great mom, but who else is she and when would that woman ever have time for me?"

All In, All Out and All Gone

Your lawn is more likely to flourish with a regular care regimen. Similarly, your dating journey will yield more results with consistent and committed efforts. This is especially true when it comes to online dating.

Posting an online profile isn't for the timid. You're essentially throwing your hat in the ring of an infinity-looped circus. Done well, it's a part-time job. Be ready to commit some time when you post, and know your limits. Don't try it during your busiest season when you're likely to miss emails and opportunities.

And don't post your profile on an Internet dating site for months at a time to flap around like an outdated event flyer. An indefinitely timed presence in the online dating world may jade you and hamper your ability to recognize that great guy when he finally comes along. Aim to focus your online dating efforts for bursts of time and then to reset with a rest period—*and update that profile a little more frequently than you do your resume!*

Shop 'Til You Drop

We'll meet the *Comparison Shopper* in Chapter Five. But you must also guard against becoming a window browser yourself.

If you opt to try online dating, periodically remind yourself that these are real people, not just advertised options in an online catalogue. With details such as hobbies, interests and career on display—as well as personal photos—it's all too easy to begin comparing one man to another like breakfast cereal. You may be exchanging emails with a guy who seems to fit what you're looking for when another better-looking or seemingly more successful man sends an inquiry—and becomes a complete distraction to exploring possibilities with the first guy. If you aren't careful, you can fall into what I view as a "trade-up" system of thinking, whereby you can become a shopper who never makes an actual purchase.

Try to view each man as a single "yes" or "no" option. Have coffee with the ones who interest you the most, but not all in the same week or you'll hinder your ability to make "yes" and "no" decisions. With one meeting, you'll know whether you might want to kiss him—and accordingly schedule a second date. Aim to only want to kiss one man at a time.

Be a Bridge Builder

Some will disagree with this idea, but I try to form friendships with some of the men I meet. A man who isn't right for me may click with one of my friends or acquaintances—or a future friend or acquaintance. It's also possible that a new guy friend will one day enable me to meet a guy I can truly develop feelings for.

This concept isn't for everyone. Not every guy I'd like to keep as a friend is able to look past an initial feeling of rejection when we both realize that a romantic relationship isn't going to happen. Friendships often last longer, so that's a shame. The men who have made permanent status on my cell phone or as Facebook friends are great guys. I consider them an unexpected bonus to my dating experience.

From the Field: *"My Friend Mike"*

"Mike" and I have an odd little history with some exceptionally bad timing. We met online, and he seemed almost normal in an overachieving, never married sort of way.

"So, have you ever even been in love?" I asked him that zinger while we dined on his back balcony one evening—slightly suspicious. *Never married?*

From best I could tell, Mike had been fairly consumed by his career and heading the HR department of a Fortune 500 company. He had lived in Europe, has an MBA from a well-known east coast school and had traveled and accomplished more by his late thirties than most do in a lifetime. Now retired and in his mid forties, he was beginning to focus on the human elements of his life.

We began spending more time together, and then somewhere around the fifth or sixth week, it got fuzzy. I think I pushed to define things and the lifelong bachelor felt pressured. Bad timing. I opted for amateurish interpreting over direct communication and made an exit, intent on enforcing "respect" on my own terms.

I soon began dating someone else, Ted, but Mike and I had so many common interests, we remained friends. Then, when Ted and I broke up for a while, Mike and I rebuilt our earlier friendship on bikes and hiking trails.

When Ted and I got together again later that year (don't get dizzy, Ted spins in and out of this a couple more times), it took Mike by surprise. While I'd grown comfortable in the fact that Mike didn't have romantic feelings for me, he had grown some, despite his initial desire to attach them to a woman who still wanted to have children.

He found out about Ted via a Facebook photo and sent me a heartfelt message. Bad timing. I read his email and wondered "what if" as I slogged forward with Ted.

Ted and I broke up again or "took a break" (Told you. Our relationship tended to get unwieldy whenever my family had a crisis, and it was an eventful couple of years). So Mike and I had dinner. It had been months since we had spoken or seen one another, and we had a lot to catch up on (I had broken off the friendship at Ted's request). At the end of the evening Mike and I found ourselves at the beginning of an "almost" kiss.

It ended quickly. Bad timing. Again. As we agreed by phone with a shared chuckle the next day, we were solid friends now. It seemed a little foolish to backtrack and risk losing that.

Ted and I ended up back together one more time. *Rinse, wash, repeat.* Mike was again a taboo friend until Ted and I broke up for good. I have no idea where Ted is now, but Mike and I are still friends, and I would never again quit a friendship to placate someone else's insecurity.

Hold on to your friendships. A life-long friend can be far more valuable than a limiting lover.

But His Profile Said...

Always remember that an online profile is a sales pitch. The realtor selling a house next to a busy freeway will emphasize the easy access to area shopping. The salesman selling a high mileage vehicle will point out the reliability of the car model. Similarly, a guy's online dating profile will feature whatever he deems to be his best selling points. There will be no disclaimer on a ten-year old photo. Full chest exposure will be more likely than full lifestyle disclosure. There are genuinely great guys out there—really! But to help you navigate past the others, here are some general translations to some common profile verbiage.

From the Field: *"Profile Translations"*

Does this thing work? / Just trying this out / My sister signed me up: "I'm embarrassed that you found this cheesy picture of me on my mountain bike if I already know you from work or something. But yeah, that's real mud. I'm really athletic and a lot of fun if you're at all interested in getting together for a drink or something."

Just looking for now / Testing the water : "I'm here for the free hors d'oeuvres and am *not* a qualified buyer."

I'm here to please you: "I want sex."

Just want some 'lovin', touchin', squeezin': Same as above, but with background music.

I'm hear to please you: "I want sex, and I can't spell."

Are there any honest women out there / Giving this one more try : "I know you'll leave me for a guy at work just like my ex—that cheating bitch—and I'll be watching you very closely."

Loves to cuddle: "Because I want sex. We get to have sex first, right?"

Honest, trustworthy, hard-working man: "Plug me in to your life, and I'll be there every night for dinner. I like to eat at 5:30. Sharp. We can go bowling on my night off after you clean up the dishes."

Please don't write unless... / Must love motorcycles, NASCAR and pit bulls: "I'm paying good money for this listing, so I don't want any junk mail. Unless you're hot...I can learn to love 'hot.'"

PLEASE READ MY PROFILE: *"I'm not talking to you, Mom, and please stop sharing this with your bingo friends. I can handle this myself.* Please, someone—anyone—confirm my existence. I've copied and pasted messages to every woman in a three county radius and got nothin'! I'll copy and paste it here on my profile again just in case you missed it: 'I need a life partner who is simple, honest and religious and who understands what I want from her...' Call me. It's OK if you're just a little bit honest and religious. We can make this work."

I'm new here to the area / Will you show me around town?: "Don't have any great date ideas, but if you do the work, I'll show up. And since I'm not really planning any of this, you're buying, OK?"

Travels frequently for business : "Don't expect too much. In fact, why don't I just call you at the last minute when I'm available? Yeah, I travel a lot. Sometimes I even fly to other cities. But I'm also able to drive across the city from my wife and kids to meet you for drinks and *dessert* occasionally."

Will treat my woman like a queen: "But make no mistake, you will be *my* woman. That's how it works. I take you to dinner. I get to keep you."

Hi: So many possibilities here… "I'm shy" or "I'm bored and there's nothing on TV tonight" or "I'm stopping there because I haven't figured out spell check" or "What more do you need? Look at my bare-chested photo—I'm a stud!" or "There…we talked. Let's have sex."

Searching for my soul mate and forever love / I'll know you when I find you: "You are perfect. You know exactly what I'm thinking and you want to do everything I want to do. Quick—what will we order for our first anniversary dinner? You don't know? Never mind. You aren't 'her.'"

Young at heart / Everyone says I look young for my age: "Unless you're ten to fifteen years younger than me, I'm really not interested. I want a really hot younger woman like that chick I dated in college that one time."

God-fearin' man seeks regular church-goin' woman: "Breakers of any of the Ten Commandments need not apply. And that time you cheated on your sixth grade math test? It counts." Alternatively, this man may be seeking a woman with a strong digestive tract who can sit through an entire Sunday morning service.

Let's just get to know each other: Could mean either "We don't have to have sex right away" or "Let's have sex immediately so we can get to know each other."

Campfire or candles?: "I'm a romantic. Tell me what works for you, and we'll have sex."

You can't always get what you want: "But hey! *I'm* still available! And I *love* the Stones. You too? Sounds like we're a match!"

Survivor / Still standing: "Well, I kind of had a drinking/ gambling/drug problem. Wife left. Lost the house and the dog. Looking for a job. But I'm pretty flexible, can drive your stick shift car and am ready to lean on YOU."

They say (insert any quote): "I have no idea what to say, so I looked up this quote online. What do you think? Wanna have sex?"

OK. I'm exaggerating. A little. But it will definitely help to keep your sense of humor and a mentally stable girlfriend handy if you engage in online dating!

CHAPTER FIVE

DEAD-END DATING

THERE ARE A FEW HIGH RISK GUYS you'll just need to walk away from. Yes, there might have been a lot of laughs over that first coffee or beer, but if you start noticing any of the red flag personas identified here—walk away. Quickly. *Before* you get sucked into a bad investment of your time.

Baggage Handlers

Bitterness, feuding and victimhood with an ex-wife will drain a new relationship faster than discovering his bachelor pad lies in mom's basement. Custody disputes, ongoing arguments over financial settlements and reimbursements, battles over transportation, trash talk, blame, jealousy, and judgment...these are but a few of the ugly manifestations of Baggage Handlers. They won't see it. Not yet. Hopefully, with time, life will mellow to "manageable," but beware of getting sucked into one of these toxic situations—and of toting around your own carry-on items...

From the Field: *"Parking Lot Apology"*

As my date liberally peppered the dinner conversation with unfriendly references to his ex-wife and I began wondering if I could get home in time to start another load of laundry, it hit me.

I think I used to sound like that!!

Oh, it was never out of context. The casual asides always fit the conversation. If the discussion was on when I would be free for dinner, I was able to slip in "of course, that's assuming my ex is on time." If music lessons were mentioned, it made sense to divulge that my ex refused to chip in on extracurricular activities. The weather? Please. We'd been married almost twenty years. I had an appropriate verbal segue for showers, sunshine and fluffy snow, as well as "cloudy with a chance of rain."

"She's a bit of a narcissist," my date was explaining as he smeared butter on a roll. "I should have known when she..."

I nodded as if I were listening and tuned out again.

How embarrassing!

The realization felt a bit like finding I'd been sporting a bit of toilet paper off the back of my heel that everyone—except me—could see. Sure, I was "over" the divorce. It had been six years, and I'd managed two long-term relationships with shelf lives of two years apiece. My ex was engaged to an old friend of mine, and it was helpful knowing that the woman hanging with my kids was unlikely to show up topless in a YouTube video. There was no question I'd been wronged. He knew it. He knew I knew it. I knew **he knew** that I knew that, basically...we had both screwed up. But while the court had thankfully stamped an ending on the marriage, we had continued our private little battle into financial reimbursements and the children's scheduling with the tenacity of finger-poking siblings sharing the back seat of a cramped sedan.

Of all people, you'd think I would have been more aware of the brevity of life having lost both parents and a grandparent just before my marriage tanked. "Is it worth the wrinkle?" was (and is) one of my favorite perspective finders. I had carpe diem-ed my way through tragedy, failure and fear. So, why the continued need to push back at my ex?

Guilt. It fed on me like a greedy tick. My ex and I had basically packed up all the bad habits of our marriage and toted them, sight unseen, into the current divorced relationship. And the tired old passive/aggressive manipulations didn't look any better in the new place.

This finally came to a head after a relationship ended, and I was forced to face the lingering effects of a tumultuous childhood that served to magnify stresses into unmanageable monsters. While scheduling my first counseling sessions, I texted "the ex".

Me: You in town?

Ex: Yes.

Me: I need to talk to you.

Ex: (Silence)

Me: In person. Can you meet me?

Ex: When?

Me: Today. Now if possible.

Ex: (Ten minute pause. I waited this time.)

Ex: OK. I can meet you at Tim Hortons in half an hour.

Me: Can't go inside. Need to talk in parking lot.

Ex: (Another lengthy pause)

Ex: Ok...

I waved him over to the passenger side door of my truck when he pulled up. He shut off his car engine, walked over through snow slush, opened the door and invaded my space. I knew he was puzzled. For the past eight years, I had barely tolerated his presence in the same room, and now I was inviting him into my enclosed vehicle.

I cracked my window a little.

After a deep breath, I began, "You probably thought I'd have a gun. You know, another one of those 'crazy ex' stories on Fox News..."

His eyebrows went up. "Um, no. I was worried something had happened to one of the kids."

Oh...! "I didn't think of that. They're fine. Sorry."

The moment had arrived. I focused on the dashboard, took a shaky breath and continued, "I am sorry, so very sorry for the way our marriage ended. I felt so alone after my parents died, and you were so busy with work and wouldn't talk to me and...but you didn't deserve to be deserted like that." Gut wrenching sobs, nose blowing, hiccups... It wasn't pretty.

Gradually, in reaching for a tissue, I shifted to face him. It was odd seeing him up close again, wearing facial expressions that I remembered on a much younger man. The divorce had aged us both. He swallowed. "Thank you. That means a lot."

I continued with more specific apologies, scraping guilt

from my life in big globs of sorrow as I smashed tissues against my wet face.

"Well, it was completely uncharacteristic of you. I know that," he said, referring to the affair that had finalized the split between us. "It was painful. Hardest thing I've ever been through. But I understand why it happened. I had pretty much stonewalled change between us. Left you on your own. And I wasn't about to budge. Our marriage wasn't good." He looked me in the eye. "It wasn't good for either of us. Or the kids... I'm sorry I treated you so badly."

My sobs launched anew, marital misery finally affirmed. Oddly, we then leisurely reminisced our dysfunction, sitting side by side there in the parking lot. It was like the slow drive-by of a freeway car wreck. Our peek into the rearview mirror didn't improve the disaster but allowed us to survey the damage as fellow survivors.

"My life is so much better now," he told me. "I'm a different man."

And I knew that to be true. While still not the man I'd choose to spend the rest of my life with, he was no longer one I needed to hide from anymore either...

We had married young, in our mid-twenties. Our engagement came within two months of our first date. We didn't have a real disagreement until our honeymoon six months later, and that was over how far to jog before breakfast. At the time, our marriage appeared as life-saving driftwood that could float me from the wreck of my childhood, but our marital harmony was based on a strong mutual ability to avoid genuine communication. Damaged people seek the familiarity of other damaged people, and we were doomed to hit a rewind on what I most hoped to avoid. When family deaths and stresses overtook us, they ran us down like a pride of lions pouncing an inattentive gazelle.

When my daughter and niece once had what I thought to be a petty disagreement, I called a forced bargaining session in an upstairs bedroom, telling the girls to come out only when they could hug one another in front of me. With a beautiful day in view outside the window, they quickly deemed the argument to be silly and performed a quick embrace for my benefit on their way outside to better things.

Sitting there in my truck as cars plowed past on the roadway in front of us, my ex and I tentatively shook hands and agreed to aim for some sort of friendship. "I'm not ready for Facebook," I told him bluntly. He laughed but accepted my connection request on LinkedIn a few days later.

And, the weight of guilt dissolved. I felt taller. Lighter. Brighter. I half-expected a balloon drop as I walked my dog later that night.

Was it truly life changing? Well, actually it was. Our lack of cooperation had been hurting me the most. I was the one who had to continually offer our kids "twenty minute early or ten minute late" drop-offs as I attempted to do a two-parent schedule by myself. I was the one whose insides twisted up over aggressive emails—*that I spitefully filed into a "Spam from Ex" folder.* Our parking lot apologies diffused the lingering almost reflexive needs to punish, control and pointedly ignore. We can now give one another grace as well as the adjoining bleacher space at our kids' sporting events.

And so, I smiled gently at my date over my pint of beer and commented, "It takes time."

"I've been divorced over a year now," he responded quickly. "Separated for two years before that. She wanted everything and couldn't agree on a fair split and…"

"That's not such a long time," I responded as he sipped his beer. "Divorce is a trauma. There's a rehab period. Too much too soon is almost a guarantee of reinjury."

"I'm not sure how to connect anymore," he admitted. "I've been on a few dates. Gotten a lot of offers, but I don't want just sex. I want the whole thing. The connection."

I nodded and commented, "Anything less isn't worth the energy." I paused and then repeated my earlier comment, "It takes time. And a bit of forgiveness in both directions. It's hard to recognize when we *aren't* ready, but I think you'll be fairly certain when you *are*."

I smiled. He sighed.

Damaged people seek the familiarity of other damaged people.

It felt like a cap and gown moment. No final answers, but I felt the strength of possibility and a commitment to continuing my education. I reached for my sweater and said a thank you. At that moment, it was clearly time to go home and tackle the pile of damp smelly towels in my laundry room.

Comparison Shoppers

He's the high school stud back on the playing field. You may feel instant chemistry with this often accomplished and dynamic man. He is deeply appreciative of your wit, your professional accomplishments and your well-toned physique. But here's the thing: He's browsing women as if they were on a dinner menu. He has a basketful of warm bread at his fingertips. It's far too soon for him to choose an entrée.

Yes, he may possibly even be "perfect." But he's not ready.

This guy simply doesn't know what he wants yet. How could he be—just out of fifteen years with a woman who suddenly went from washing his socks to taking him to the cleaners? He needs to make a few dating mistakes: the unrelatable younger woman (*Madonna who?*), the entrancing goddess who has nothing to say after her verbal replay of the week's best reality TV, the no-strings bed partner... Nice, normal You won't look good until he's been burned a few times and is ready for *real*. He's seen the good, bad and butt-ugly end of a marriage. Expecting him to recognize quality before he's dated a quantity of women is like peddling your heart at a flea market.

From the Field: "*Awkward Dance Moves*"

Bonnie and I met on a dance floor. We kind of bumped into each other, she said, "I know you!" and we realized our kids had attended the same private school in our previous more privileged lives. We clicked and became fast friends. Odd scenario, but totally true. She's hauled me home from surgery—"*I really suck at this nursing stuff, you know. Are you going to throw up?*"—and I hold her beer bottle whenever an AC/DC song pulls her irresistibly into her classic 80's hair flipping dance moves.

One night last summer, we scanned our dive bar of choice—chosen for the danceability of the evening's band—with no serious hopes of meeting eligible men in a venue where we'd basically be lip reading. We were there to dance. It's great cardio, and we always laugh a lot. Which is a lot more fun than schlepping through perpetual first dates.

"I don't know..." Bonnie was concerned at the sparse turnout. But then the lead singer of Longreef, who looked as if he'd just toweled off from a salty dip in Australia's Coral Sea, started chatting with us, and it was game on. Bonnie is a talented, natural flirt, who can electrify conversations with casual arm touches. The singer hovered, and it was a fun chat.

The room filled quickly with an eclectic assortment of the trashy and the classy, and once the band started up, Bonnie and I moved into the dancing crowd, pausing only for occasional sips of beer and water.

"Oh. I remember him. He's a good dancer." It was dark, but I figured out which guy Bonnie meant as he danced his way over and swiveled his hips in our direction. She was right. He wasn't an awkward offbeat swayer; he really moved well. Fairly quickly, however, he moved in on me.

"Wow. You work out don't you?" He glanced toward my stomach. "When you dance I can see your abs against your shirt."

The shirt wasn't tight. I wasn't sure how to respond. Bonnie stood nearby, smiling awkwardly. Steve wore the confident smile of a seasoned pro, accustomed to getting first pick of the room. He seemed intent on closing the space between us as quickly as possible.

"I need some water. Want some, Bonnie?"

She gave me a hesitant nod, and I fled, feeling a little guilty.

Mental telepathy: "I love you Bonnie! You already know him, right? I just really have to pee, and why the hell is he commenting on my abs?!"

I took my time in the bathroom and then grabbed a couple of waters on my way back to the dance floor. The music was good, and I wriggled my way back in, contritely handing Bonnie her ice water.

"So, do you live nearby? We should get together sometime."

I struggled to answer. Bonnie shrugged her shoulders and looked away. Amused.

"Nah. Other side of town really. Great band, huh?"

I looked to Bonnie for a contribution, and she bailed.

"Bathroom," she motioned with a grin.

Chastised and abandoned, I danced on with Steve. When the song ended, I indicated that I needed to check on Bonnie. I knew she was fine, and that she would also be fine with being my designated excuse to ditch Steve and figure out our exit plan.

"Don't leave without telling me. Promise? I'll walk you to your car. Don't leave without giving me your number!" He pressed his fingers to my shoulder. "Promise me." He was handsome and would undoubtedly enhance a photo, but he exuded a desperate sort of charm.

He's on autopilot, Heather.

I'm not sure what an expression of pity, compassion, tactfulness and revulsion looks like—it's not one I practice in the bathroom mirror—but I'm fairly sure I hit it dead on.

Ick.

Be a grownup!

"Thanks Steve, but we may need to scoot out of here."

He frowned and wheedled. I gave him a little wave over my shoulder.

A couple of soccer dad types slowed my progress toward

the bathroom, where I suspected/hoped I might find Bonnie. But their smokers' breath affirmed my launch comment to Bonnie as we began our evening, "Let's not worry about guys tonight, OK? Let's just have fun dancing."

The set ended as I found her, leaning against a bathroom wall.

"What do you think? Steve is kind of aggressive…"

"Yeah. He's a good dancer. Danced a lot with him last time I was here. Think he's kind of a regular."

We looked at each other. Bonnie winced. "Band's great, but my feet hurt!"

I laughed. "Told you!" I'm permanently sensible on my heel height following two ankle surgeries. Bonnie pushes it up a couple of inches.

"Done?"

She winced again and tried to massage her left foot through the black strappy wedge that had abused it. "Are you OK with that?"

"Absolutely."

"Are you sure?"

"Yes! The only question is…"

"What?!" she groaned. Once Bonnie's feet are done, not even Bon Jovi will move her musical muse. She smiled through her pain to show she was kidding.

"Steve… He wanted to say goodbye." I shrugged. "I think he's kind of creepy. But I don't want to be mean."

Bonnie snorted and tipped her head. "Mean?! You?! Let's just go. He'll live. Don't know if my feet will, though!"

We ran into a high school friend on the way out.

"I think this is the *last* place I saw you, Terri! At our high school reunion! How've you been?"

"Same. Great. You know." She gave a weary, lips-only smile. "But that guy you were dancing with? Steve…"

I nodded.

"Bad news. He's slept with just about every woman here."

I didn't ask. Didn't want to know. "Thanks. We were just dancing. But Bonnie—Oh! (I quickly introduced them)—and I, we're taking off. Good to see you again, Terri."

She nodded and turned away. Bonnie and I edged quickly toward the door, politely brushing off the soccer dads.

"Do you think he saw us? Did we make it?"

"Ow. Ow. Ow. Ow. Ow…"

That was Bonnie. Limping all the way to my car, which was unfortunately parked at the far edge of the lot. But I knew her feet would probably feel better in the morning than whomever Steve took home that night.

Bottom Dwellers

These men are the anecdotes of tomorrow, the antiheroes of dating horror tales your best friends will chime in on as shared survival stories.

These guys are basically looking for sex and/or a surface level, low pressure/no pressure relationship. Consider this man to be a cold front looking for a warm bed. Anything more or less than that will send them scurrying for cover where they'll simply lurk to await another unwitting or gullible female. This guy won't remember your name for longer than two weeks and will hesitate before saying it aloud.

I won't pretend to understand the underpinnings of these guys—snicker if you must—but those "underpinnings" are what drive the dump truck.

They may push your boundaries a little. Or a lot. A friend of mine felt pressured into sexting within a couple of dates. It felt wrong but she felt helpless to stop. I think she knew her edgy "Biker Guy" would delete her if she quit—another case of neediness taking someone down the wrong road. Too much too soon on the physical side will blow any semblance of relational balance quickly and—*without fail*—leave you feeling poorly about your choices and yourself.

My friend Danielle says I read people well. I think that has helped me to (mostly) avoid the Bottom Dwellers. I do remember a major misread, though.

Massage Man had passed through my Match.com email filtering process with a few short but witty responses. He commented on my intelligence rather than my butt, which put him a mile ahead of the rest of my inbox that week. But very soon, after we had agreed to lunch at a Chinese restaurant, he began integrating talk of his in-home massage table. When I was unable to lightly deflect and divert him from the topic of body oils, I bluntly told him that he was making me uncomfortable. He immediately backed off and apologized, explaining that it was a therapeutic thing he really believed in, but that he understood my discomfort. Done and done, right?

Nah. As we chopsticked our way through lunch a couple of afternoons later and I attempted to draw him out whilst he smiled seductively across the Formica table top, the truth finally came out.

I like to think that my genuineness abraded his veneer

down to where traces of a gentleman remained.

As I gulped ice water, Massage Man shifted uncomfortably, unwilling to meet my eyes. "Say um, Heather…? You seem like a nice lady. I should probably tell you that I'm not exactly looking for what I said in my profile." He went on to describe what he was seeking: basically, a female with my physical attributes but with a long-term view that extended just shy of seven hours. Toothbrush optional.

I thanked him for both the lunch and his candor. And scurried for the door.

Friends of mine who have dated Bottom Dwellers usually have a torrid and insecure couple of weeks followed by cold quiet regret. They often have aspirations of growing these intellectually stunted little boys into adult men. I don't see the point of expending that sort of energy on someone who, at best, is going to drag his feet the whole way and scuff up your good life. I've tried to avoid Bottom Dwellers completely.

From the Field: *"Moving Target"*

"TallTom" was eager to meet. His online profile had a lot of the right components: a strong work ethic, a love of travel and an apparent compassion for others (He listed "volunteering" as an interest). He was a former college athlete still committed to personal fitness. I decided he was worth a coffee. We exchanged phone numbers.

He happened to be near my gym as I was lifting one

Saturday morning, so I agreed to meet him at the Tim Horton's next door when I finished. A refresher glance at his profile before walking over revealed him to be only thirty-six years old—beneath my preferred age range. I wiped some sweat from my face and noticed I'd chipped a nail.

Strikes two and three. Maybe you should just drive home...

Mustering my best "let's get this over with" attitude, I trudged into the empty restaurant. The counter guy was ready.

"What can I get for you?"

"Umm, I'm meeting someone." I glanced around at vacant tables. "Is there anyone else here?" I nodded towards the restrooms.

He shrugged, his mind already on an English paper or Algebra homework. "No. Just you."

*Bananas, bagels, deli meat...*I began planning my trip to the grocery five minutes down the road.

He looked out at the parking lot. "Does he drive a Jeep?"

Moments later, the door swung open and a tall leathery-tanned man walked in. We smiled at one another. "Tom?" He nodded and walked over.

He towered over me, almost too distant for me to decide whether he was attractive or not. I figured I'd find out within the next sentences. He ordered two coffees.

We sat down by the fireplace and began.

"Hey. You look great. So you were just at the gym? What did you do?"

"Upper body. Back and biceps today. Walked on the track. Have to wait a little bit longer on the fun stuff." I nodded toward my lower right leg, which was encased at that time in a surgical walking boot. *He has a nice smile. Is he a maybe?*

Thirty-six. Don't think so.

"So, how much longer do you have that thing on?" He reached a hand over to touch my fingers. "I like your skin," he said.

I must have looked puzzled. "You're really fit," he commented. "I like that."

"Thanks. So you live in Dublin," I asked, ignoring the skin comment because I didn't understand it at all.

"Yeah. But I'm getting some work done at the house—installing closet organization systems in two spare bedrooms. So, I'm staying at the Hilton over there. I always stay there." He nodded toward the fireplace behind us.

"You're doing a lot of renovations?"

"Oh, you know. Floors, countertops—always something."

"And you always move out to the Hilton?"

"My cousin is the manager. He always gives me a good deal on a room."

He grabbed hold of my fingers. "We could go watch a movie. It's really nice. I like you. I really like older women."

My brain screeched a warning. I extricated my fingers, deploying them to scratch a non-itchy shoulder, and dropped my hand to my lap. "I don't do that."

He looked puzzled. "Watch movies? You don't watch movies? Is it against your religion or something?" He grinned at me.

I shook my head. "I don't know you. Why would I ever go to your hotel room?"

"I'll be good. It's just a good place to relax and watch a movie, you know?"

I told him I needed to get home to let my dog out.

"But I'm leaving for Florida tomorrow. Two weeks. Vacation."

"Sounds great." I tipped my head at the snowy parking lot. "Good for you. Hope you have a great time." I rose to leave.

"I'll walk you to your car."

"That isn't necessary."

He followed anyway and tried to kiss me by the driver's side door. "That's my gym!" I protested, nodding toward the building as I pushed him away, thankful that there were indeed people in the parking lot. "You're in really good shape," he said, teetering forward.

"Gotta go!" I reached for the door handle, an index finger on my car remote's alarm button.

"You sure you don't want to watch a movie?"

"You're kind of used to getting what you want, aren't you?"

He laughed uncomfortably. By now I was seated, injured leg extended, ripping apart the Velcro-ed straps. *There are no quick get-aways for women wearing surgical walking boots.* I held the heavy boot between us as I closed the door. He turned toward his Jeep, and I headed for the grocery.

I didn't expect to hear from him again, but as I logged on to read Match.com emails at 7:20 the next morning, my phone rang. "Come over," he told me. "We can have breakfast."

"No." I didn't sugarcoat it this time.

"I leave for vacation tomorrow. Will be gone for two weeks. I thought we could get to know each other a little better."

I ended the call and texted Danielle. She called as I made

my next discovery.

"Wow. His profile just came up as having looked at mine. And it says he lives in Westerville, not Dublin."

"Eww… Basic scumbag."

We confirmed her diagnosis when TallTom relocated yet again and became a Florida resident on Match.com the following day.

"Palm Harbor?! Can't believe I wasted thirty minutes sipping coffee with a fake man when I could have been sampling cheeses at the grocery!"

Danielle laughed. I deleted TransientTallTom's phone number.

Skimmers

Skimmers can be very pleasant people but may bore you into your own rude "I gotta get out of here" behavior. Let's hope not. These gentlemen lack discernible depth and personality. This is usually obvious via an email exchange at your online dating venue of choice or while they make small talk at the gym. But occasionally, one will slip through all filters, which is why I prefer quick meet-and-greets to first dates. *It's far easier to extend a drink than to prematurely end a dinner.*

You will want to like him. There will be nothing to dislike. The problem is: It may be difficult to get a grip on any element of this spray mist of a personality.

Yes, I feel a little catty typing these words. Skimmers are fine people! But do I want to endure hours of silent dining experiences? *Oops, forgot about the clanking of forks against plates and the occasional unfortunate slurp.*

No thank you.

If you are seeking to live expansively, to learn and grow in a consistent manner—choosing a nice man who cares for nothing but his job and his girl will suck the life out of you! Nice equals stable, but stable does not necessarily equal *right fit*. Stable is only one element in a good relationship choice. We get confused on this, particularly after we've encountered a Bottom Dweller or two!

From the Field: *"Coffee to Go"*

He was early and eager. I glanced up from the restaurant booth I'd commandeered as a remote office that morning and hit "save" on an in-progress article as he squinted in my direction.

"Heather?" His hesitant smile grew into a high beam grin when I nodded a greeting, and he slid into the opposite side with a plateful of pastry and steaming mug of coffee.

"Strudel."

"Smells good."

"It's the cinnamon."

We shook hands and nodded to acknowledge our shared appreciation of cinnamon.

"How's your morning going?" I asked, with instant knowledge that our little meet-and-greet would go no further. He seemed pleasant but was much older than I'd expected. And he knew it. His smile had an apologetic, "Yeah, I kinda used a ten-year old photo for my online profile" element to it. But there was also a hint of delight at having lured me in.

Internally, I sighed. "So, you're in client services?"

He worked on his pastry, dropping crumbs onto the tabletop, and explained that he used to be. "I guess I should have updated that," he grinned. "I left that job a couple of years ago. I'm more of an IT guy now."

He continued to grin at me as he chewed. I reached for my emptied coffee mug, set it down... My water glass held only melting slivers of ice and the blueberry breakfast bagel was also long gone. There was little to do but muscle through a conversation. I grabbed the wadded up napkin from my plate and wiped at a spot on the table.

"I already ate," I said. "So...you like to travel."

He nodded, adding a smile as he furtively reached for a flake of pastry dangling to the right of his mouth. I'd been on standby to do the pantomime hint but was glad he'd found it himself. Crumb gesturing seemed far too intimate and would have conflicted with my new and immediate goal of expanding the space between us.

"Not for a while," he managed, stuffing the last three bites of breakfast into his mouth. More flakes flew toward the tabletop. I determinedly held his gaze and ignored them. "Not since my last job. Went to Europe right after college when I was in my twenties, though."

I nodded politely but was unwilling to prop up the conversation with a follow up question.

"So, you're working?" He nodded toward my laptop.

"Yeah, just finishing an article. Due this afternoon." I spotted a potential plausible ending to our appointment. "Hope I can get it finished in time! Kind of a tight deadline," I hinted, glancing longingly toward my MacBook blinking sympathetically beside me.

He grinned and sipped down the last of his coffee. "So, you like to travel too?"

Damn. My polite hint hadn't carried enough weight for impact. "Yes, I do." I nodded. "Hoping I can get caught up on work before we leave for vacation next week!" I glanced meaningfully at my laptop.

"Where are you going?" He appeared to be fully caffeinated. Perky. There was a savvy sort of gleam in his eye.

He knows you're trying to get rid of him, Heather.

"Colorado."

He nodded as if he'd heard of it.

I smiled, trying to think of a way to end the non-conversation. He smiled back at me. We nodded at one another, holding the smiles in silence because we had nothing to say. It was now impossible to determine which one of us was more boring, but I was definitely the most bored.

He leaned against the back of his seat and stretched.

The breakfast booth was basically my base camp, with note cards and papers strewn alongside my laptop. I had planned on working there until it was time to leave for a lunch appointment on the other side of town. Basically, I had invited this gentleman into my "office," lacked the means to make my own quick exit and now had a squatter. He glanced towards the coffee machine.

"Want a refill on that?" He nodded at my empty mug.

My stomach lurched. I debated telling him that I needed to go, but in my email message, I had said I'd be working at my "remote office" all morning and that he was welcome to stop by around 9am for a few minutes. He reached for my mug, and I yanked it back.

"I've had enough already. Thanks."

He picked up his own mug, and I quickly caught his eye. "I really appreciate you driving over to meet me this morning." I nodded toward my laptop. "I really need to get back to writing that article, but thank you for coming!"

Thank you for coming?? That was bad, Heather.

He flinched and grabbed his jacket. He left his plate and empty mug on the table, embarrassed. It was mutual.

The "Maybe Married" and "Currently Separated"

This is basically a game of "let's pretend": "Let's pretend he's physically and legally free," "Let's pretend he's emotionally available," "Let's pretend there's going to be a happy ending on this…"

Dating sites often allow men and women to classify themselves as "currently separated." These guys are aching to know what's out there. The home life is crappy, and they've heard stories from their single buddies or watched too many beer commercials. Mid-life crisis? Perhaps. Just don't let it become your crisis.

I speak from sad and painful experience. "Separated" does not equal "divorced." There will be reasons or excuses: finances, the kids, she's not stable (and they never have sex anyway), it's "in process…" I'm sure there are more—these are just the ones I've heard from friends and would-be boyfriends. These men are living in the fringes of two worlds, either trying to "have it all" or unsure of what it is they, in fact, want. This is the behavior of a weak man who is unable to stand on his own or simply lacks the courage to be decisive. He's like a timid Tarzan, attempting a through-the-jungle vine swing, but unable to release his backwards grip. And so he dangles helplessly, holding onto two women at the same time, looking at you with woeful longing eyes.

A) If he isn't divorced, he isn't available. B) If he is planning a divorce, he's still tied to a wife! This man needs a lot—conversation, reassurance, hope, sex—but is not yet able to give. How fun and fulfilling will that ever be? When mom said, "clean up as you go?" That applied to a lot more than kitchen countertops.

One relationship at a time, mister.

From the Field: *"Long Shot Lover"*

We ordered from the sushi menu and then relaxed, sipping ice waters on the street side patio of a downtown Columbus restaurant.

"It is sooo good to see you! You look amazing!"

There was a euphoria to our reunion, this instant transport back to simpler times when boys had been the biggest complications in our young lives. Yolanda and I had been sorority sisters at Indiana University. She had emailed she'd be in town for a couple of days, and I excitedly typed her into my calendar.

"Can't believe it's been over twenty years!"

Yolanda started to focus on the chair beside me in concentration.

"No, don't do the math. I don't want to know!" I laughed.

"Aww, we were cute then. We're still damn cute now."

We toasted ourselves with an affirming clink.

As we ran through names of friends and brought one another up-to-date on what we knew of our former housemates, there was a level of comfort between us that had eluded me as a careful, less confidant sorority girl. Yolanda's poise had been a birthright, while my own had grown only as I slowly refocused my fears about what other people thought of me into an ever-growing curiosity about who those people might be themselves.

I asked about Yolanda's high-powered job and her high-maintenance dogs. Eventually we got to our love lives.

"Nada. Not dating anyone right now," I said. "There have been a few first dates, but no one has made the cut yet."

"I thought…"

"That ended a few months ago. How about you, Yolanda?"

The sushi had arrived. She took a minute to dip a piece of yellowfin tuna into the wasabi-amped soy sauce. "Well…" she began before popping it into her mouth, slowly chewing and swallowing.

"It's complicated. I'm visiting him here in town actually. It's long distance." She glanced up at me. "He's still married."

"Yikes. That's a tough road, Yolanda." She knew my history included a dip to the dark side. With the conviction of a reformed ex-smoker, I now spend a lot of time educating women sucked into the endless emptiness of affairs on the realities of such a situation.

She spent a few minutes describing him: educated, confident, attractive, witty, and accomplished. "He's everything I want." She twirled her straw around the lime slice in her water glass.

"Everything except 'available...'"

She sighed. "I know. It wasn't supposed to go on this long. He's had some family issues and couldn't disengage yet."

"It's never supposed to go on that long, Yolanda. But these men are weak. They lack the ability to be decisive and end up hurting their families and the woman they make promises to."

She didn't say anything.

"It's tough to live your life on hold for someone like that! You end up living for brief moments instead of creating a life you want to live in full-time!" *Too much, Heather.* "I'm sorry," I added softly.

She shook her head at my apology. Even now, for a truly accomplished professional woman like Yolanda, boys—or "a boy"—could still be the biggest "complication."

"How long are you going to give this, Yolanda?"

She shrugged. "Can't do it much longer. It hurts."

Cling Wrap Men

While excellent for preventing splatters in the microwave and filling your fridge with decomposing leftovers, cling wrap in human form is completely stifling.

This is the man who will fall in love with you before he knows your middle name, the guy who is interested in matching himself to your life—"*I LOVE museums/racquetball/whatever you just said*"—and who plans for the holidays after one good kiss. He is needy and you represent his life preserver. He may lavish you with compliments and praise, but does he know you? Really know you? Consider how empty a man must be to decisively choose a woman he has yet to discover. He will follow you like a puppy dog, be jealous of your friends and try to pin you down on travel plans for next summer. Your friends may notice you deflating like a punctured balloon as this man encircles your life in a bear hug that leaves you no breathing room.

I used to think this issue could be worked through as a couple. I now suspect that cling wrap tendencies can be indicative of lingering post-divorce trauma or even insecurities that may have afflicted his marriage. This man is wounded and needs to heal himself before he can be a whole man with you.

From the Field: *"Vacuum Packed"*

"Um… do you want to go grab the dog food, while I start on produce?"

He leaned on the cart and smiled at me. "No, I like watching you pick out tomatoes."

I gulped and mustered a smile. "OK. Don't know what's so special about me and tomatoes, but let's get it done!"

His eyes softened. "I like watching you do just about anything, Heather."

The truth was I needed a bit of breathing room, and this guy always needed mouth-to-mouth, inhaling everything I had whether it was my time, thoughts or activities.

"Are you sure you don't need to pick up anything for yourself?

"No," he smiled. "I'm just here to hang out with you."

Of course, I ran it past Danielle the next day. "Am I

wrong to feel this way?"

"He's just way more into you than you are into him, Heather. I dated a guy like that once. Wonderful guy, but it always felt like 'too much.'"

"That's it—the 'too much' part. And I *know* he needed other groceries! He ended up getting a few of the same items I picked out, but it's like he wouldn't mention his *own* shopping list for fear I wouldn't accompany him to the other side of the store! How do I do this, Danielle? I do care about him. I keep thinking with a little more time, it will settle down a little, but this is hard!"

"I don't think you can count on him backing off, Heather. And if he keeps crowding you, you'll lose respect for him pretty fast. Can't you just say something?"

"I've tried a couple of times—said that I'm used to having a little 'alone' time and that I'm sure he has stuff he needs to take care of too. He nods his head really quickly like it doesn't bother him, which means it bothers him a *lot*! And then I feel badly and start trying to include him all the time again." I slumped. "I'm afraid to say 'no,' and it's sucking the life out of this relationship!"

"How long has he been divorced?"

"Well, he's past the two-year mark now, but we started dating when he was barely a year out—which is why we've been up and down so much, I think."

"Or it may just be who he is, Heather."

"Or who he is with me..."

Deadbeats

Meeting the guy on location for your first meet-and-greet is smart, but if he asks you to drive him home because his friend won't be back to pick him up for another hour? Possible deadbeat—or worse.

POF actually includes home and car ownership in its profile listings. Too bad there isn't also a credit rating...

Deadbeats will be very interested in your financial success—*and not so interested in picking up the check*. His lack of cash isn't the issue. The expectation that he will spend quantities of yours could be a problem, however.

Some very nice guys are forced to live paycheck to paycheck for a while following a divorce, so don't be a deadbeat yourself. Try not to let a guy spend too much on a first meeting—limit his investment to a single drink with the option to add an appetizer if merited. Grownup singles do not take advantage of other singles.

From the Field: *"Need Meets Greed"*

She arched an eyebrow. "Clue number one: When you can't send him a birthday card because he has no mailing address. Number two would be when he doesn't have a professional email address. And number three? When he tells you he's an alcoholic." Linda shook her head and reached for the wine. "Jim wasn't my best decision."

Linda is a sharp, down-to-earth attorney. Smart. Attractive.

"How?" I asked.

She sipped and thought for a moment. "Well... The guy

I was in love with got married to someone else. It wasn't a great time in my life. I was in my thirties. Working all the time. And then I got a bad—and unfair—performance review. So I went out drinking with a girlfriend. The Browns were playing the Steelers. A guy sent us drinks and then worked his way over."

"Jim?"

"Uh huh. My friend said, 'No way—he's a Steelers fan,' but I was lonely and took him home. Didn't really expect anything to come of it. He ended up moving in when I figured out he was taking turns living with his mom and his sister..."

"Yikes. And he actually told you he had a drinking problem?"

"Yep. It came up one night when we were toasted in a bar. Kind of a 'by the way, you might want to know I'm an alcoholic...'"

She shrugged. "I figured I could help him."

Linda and I were seated at a high top at one of our favorite happy hour spots, saving seats for two girlfriends who would join us later. Though the bar hummed, we'd found a quiet bubble for conversation.

"How bad did it get?"

"Well, I basically supported him. He would buy me wonderful gifts. But pay for them with my money. I started hiding my checks and credit cards, but he always found them. Like he said, he was an alcoholic—and he needed alcohol. I remember one Christmas—we were in Florida with my family—he gave me a $60 bottle of wine and a spa package. All to impress my family but paid for by yours truly. I had to tell the bank not to cash my checks no matter what he said—embarrassing. My friends couldn't really figure it out. They thought he had to be good in bed." She shook her head. "Not the case."

"Linda! I can't believe you stayed with him!"

"I know. Me neither. Like I said, it was a bad time. I was lonely. Had told a friend I was going to 'find me a man,' and well... Be careful what you wish for!"

She leaned in. "You know the worst thing? *Besides* when he'd *sell* the jewelry he had bought for me with MY money to buy more alcohol?"

I waited.

"I married him. Lasted ten years." She shook her head slowly with a wry grimace. "Haven't really felt the urge to get married again."

Vacationers

He behaves similarly to the Comparison Shopper, but this man's motives are completely different. The Vacationer is facing significant life challenges and is basically looking for a break from real life. He's still battling with an ex-wife or struggling with financial and custody issues. He is seeking diversion. You want connected conversation over candlelight; he just wants the Happy Meal. "To go."

Ultimately, this man may want more—a life partner, even. But, he can't handle "more" while he's handling the downsizing of his dreams. This guy has a journey in front of him, but he has yet to shoulder his own backpack. He may appreciate your sympathy and your wisdom, but he's hurting and unable to wash the wound yet.

This may be the guy you will wish you had met five years later, but we can't help timing. Wish him well and point him toward the trailhead.

From the Field: *"Disappearing Date"*

"Umm... my kids might come over tomorrow. I have to go to the grocery and..."

I could hear some background noise. He had mentioned something about going to the hardware store on his way home from work. "Oh."

"So...how are you doing? How's the ankle healing and...?"

"Fine thanks." I wanted to keep it positive and figured I'd better get off the phone quickly.

Corey was the first guy I'd wanted a second date with in several months. I thought it was mutual. He had blushed a couple of times during our first lunch—usually a good sign. He'd called and texted frequently, but had this bad habit of disappearing on date day. I hesitated at typing him onto my calendar the third time, but I wanted to kiss him.

So I lingered. He was smart and attractive. I liked his voice. But he was dealing with some big stuff: an ex-wife who had cheated and then burdened him with two mortgages after the divorce. Court dates for custody issues. She had a serious illness, and he rarely saw his kids. I knew these things...and I knew that his divorce was fresh—one year out, in fact. He was angry, and life was unfair. And yet I lingered because I wanted to kiss him.

My friends knew my struggle. "Hear anything?"

"Nah. I deleted him again."

"Good."

"But I still like him, dammit."

And then the dearly deleted would text me again.

I sympathized. My own divorce had been horrible, lengthy and grueling. I understood his desperate minute-to-minute lifestyle. And I let that get in the way of what I knew to be true.

It was simply too soon. Too soon for him to be dating anybody, much less a woman who was past all of that stuff and knew what still lay ahead for him.

We had a couple more dates. He was an OK kisser. I'd have kissed him again. But ultimately I watched him spiral away, knowing I was seeing him at one of life's lowest points and that "bottom" still lay ahead. Wondering where he'd land when he scaled the challenges and knowing that I'd never find out.

A few years ago, I'd have "vacationed" with him and tried to help do the things he needs to do himself, but I've grown selective about where I spend my energy.

Good guy, wrong time, bad fit.

Damaged Souls

Chances are you won't even be tempted into a second date with this guy unless you have what my friend Sarah wryly refers to as "the social worker gene." You may want to pass on the name of your therapist and proffer a tissue, but this guy is living in the past. He's angry or he's devastated. He's guilt-ridden. His wife is a bitch or a saint. It's his fault or her fault—not *their* fault. There is no perspective because he's still wallowing in the middle of a mess.

Be kind, but do not get sucked into coffee counseling unless you've a strong deflecting mechanism for all the negative energy this guy exudes.

If you *do* venture into any sort of relationship with this guy, hoist up your confidence and pin it in place. The sensitivities of a Damaged Soul remind me of a fragile tooth, vulnerable to the slightest changes in temperature. You may be required to determine if/why/when he is offended. You will wonder why he doesn't just speak his mind, but remember that it's engaged elsewhere or even temporarily lost.

From the Field: *"The Bedroom Door"*

Sometimes the damage goes deep and causes adult relationships to wobble and topple from atop the cracked foundations of a warped childhood.

Ryan walked in five minutes early and found me hunched over my laptop in a coffee shop booth. We shook hands and he slid in on the opposite side.

"You look great."

I thanked him for the standard "thank God you resemble your profile photo" greeting and asked him how his day was going.

He frowned. "Had to talk to the ex father-in-law. We're kind of *still* in business together..."

"That could get kind of awkward."

He nodded and shared the whole story. Pressured into a

marriage that included a great family business opportunity. The unfulfilling marriage had fizzled out completely when his now ex-wife hooked up with an old high school boyfriend. He blamed her for everything and called her a "class A bitch." But her daddy still signed his paychecks... Didn't sound like he got along with his mother too well either, but that seemed the safer topic, so I asked about his family.

"Well," he shifted uncomfortably. "It really started when... Shit, I shouldn't be telling you this stuff."

I waited.

"You see. OK, this is *not* normal. When I was a teenager, doing what teenage boys do, if you know what I mean... Well, I was kind of going to town in my room, bed squeaking, and I look up right at the moment of—you know—*and I see my mom peeking in the doorway!* She had cracked open the door and was watching me jack off in my bed!"

I sipped my water calmly, mentally crossed Ryan off as a possibility for Friday night and pressed forward.

"Did you ever talk to her about it?"

"Shit no! And it's been weird ever since." Judging from his age, I tabulated a good thirty years of "weird."

"Do you talk at all?"

"I was finally down in Florida near my folks last March. Staying in a hotel. Mom talked me into moving over to their house. It was cheaper, so I decided to try again." He paused dramatically. "But it was more weirdness!" He shifted and leaned forward on the table. "OK, you're an advice columnist. Explain this.

"First off, I'm taking a shower, and she keeps yanking the bath rug out from under the bathroom door. It didn't really fit under there and made the door not close properly, so I pulled it back in. I get out of the shower, and it's yanked out again!" He shook his head in disbelief. "But there's more! A client called me late at night. So, wanting to be quiet—that house is like a damn museum!—I took the call outside and wandered down the street a bit. When I hung up and turned to walk back to Mom and Dad's, I see my mom. Standing in her bathrobe at the end of the driveway...staring me down *like a goddamn ghost!* As soon as I took a step, she turned and ran. I watched the houselights go dark as I came up the driveway. And when I tried to go in the front door—it was locked!"

He didn't need anything from me and chugged on forward to the pinnacle of his dysfunctional horror story. "I found a key and got in, but that night, I was frustrated as hell. I got in bed and—you know—I started to relieve myself. And..." He looked at me, "I can't believe I'm telling you this shit."

Silent agreement.

"Once again, as I'm climaxing, I look to the door—which I had made *sure* was closed—and it was cracked open again! And I can see my mom's eyes looking in!" He slammed a palm on the table. "I packed my stuff in the morning and haven't talked to either one of them since."

I pondered my next words carefully, recognizing that they would probably be amongst my last to this would-be date.

"Is your mom kind of obsessive/compulsive? You know, everything has to be 'just so?' You said 'museum'..."

"Oh yeah. That's my mom. You don't lay anything down without her swooping in to pick it up." He shook his head at the thought, and then grinned at me. "So when do you want to go kayaking?"

"Wait… Is it possible that she's simply attempting to maintain her idea of order?"

He shook his head. "Mom? She's nuts."

"Might be. But think about it. The bathmat. It has a specific place to be in that bathroom. She was afraid you wouldn't remember to put it back and just had to fix it herself. Maybe…?"

He shrugged. "But locking me out of the house? Give me a reason for that."

"She was nosey. Embarrassed to be caught, so she raced back in, hoping you didn't see her and, in her panic, automatically locked the door on her way."

He softened slightly. "Well maybe." The angry eyes returned. "But sneaking around to watch me in my bedroom?! As a fifteen-year old kid and then as a fifty-year old man?!"

"Disturbing," I agreed. "But how would she feel about an unannounced stranger in her house? Is it possible that she heard noises and crept around to see if you'd brought some unknown woman into her pristine home?"

Ryan's face shifted from doubt to deep thought to a slow realization. "Wait…you could be right. The bed was squeaking. And when I was a kid. Same thing. She was so worried one of us would get a girl pregnant or something. Damn! She isn't nuts. She's just nosy and controlling as hell!"

I nodded. "Sounds more likely."

He looked me in the eye. "I can't believe I've told you all of this, but do you realize I spent my whole life until now convinced she was some kind of pervert?"

He sat up. "I have to call her. Seriously. I didn't even

call on Mother's Day this year. Thanks for listening. This has been great! Want to go kayaking next weekend?"

I made an excuse.

Primitive Islands

He's new to dating and unsure of how to connect. He was probably shocked by the collapse of his marriage: a partnership that played out as parallel lives with no connecting communication. His idea of conversation won't extend deeper than rudimentary chat. His bar is low because he has yet to experience true emotional connection.

Give it a try if he professes a desire to build intimacy and you're truly motivated to work with him. But understand, that what feels momentous to him will feel minimal to you if you've had a previous connected relationship. It will be uphill, and he may be tempted to pause indefinitely on a plateau because, again, the view will be better than anything he's known before. The question will always be: Is it good enough for you?

From the Field: *"Cheese and Crackers"*

Jim: You here yet?

Me: Yep. Near the cheese counter.

Me: And I see carrots. Produce department is to the right.

He was late by fifteen minutes. When my phone vibrated with his text, I'd been edging toward the cash registers, debating whether the veggie crisps would be worth a checkout line wait.

Jim: Left phone in car and couldn't find you. On my way back in.

Moments later he appeared, propped over an empty grocery cart that, next to his weightlifter physique, looked like a kid-sized toy. We recognized one another from our online profile photos, and Jim's face lit up. "Heather?"

I nodded and smiled.

"You are so cute." He was pleased.

I felt like the doll that might fit in his grocery cart seat.

"Um. Thanks. Wondered if we'd ever find each other in here!"

"I left my phone in my car," he explained again.

I nodded. Smiled again.

"Damn. You're so cute."

We were temporarily stuck.

"Nice grocery, huh? I haven't been in here before."

"They have a great deli/carryout. C'mon, I'll show you."

He led me back by the cheese department where we divvied up the display sample—he took the cranberry crackers; I took the Fontina cheese—to purchase and share on a potential future date (he was handsome enough for hope). When we reached the deli counter he requested samples of a couple of his favorite sides for me to taste while he ordered dinner for his kids.

During our subsequent short wander through the aisles, I could reach no conclusion. Our conversation was limited to commentaries on grocery items. I was pretty sure we could order off the same menu, but wondered what we'd do when we weren't chewing. He exuded an elemental sexuality that merited a second look, however. After all, my cheese needed to sit on his cranberry crackers.

We were both exceptionally busy, and I had no free evenings in the foreseeable future, so we met for a quick lunch and then, on another afternoon, we walked at a favorite park.

He huffed his way up and down a couple of hills—not as into the walking as much as he was the talking. Which was fine. We stood and talked at the bottom of a wooded rise.

He spilled a little of his inner turmoil regarding the death of his marriage. His wife had cheated and was ignoring their two children in favor of playing with her new boyfriend. He worried about his kids. "See? Isn't she gorgeous?" He showed me a phone photo of his cheerleader daughter. "And here's Chad…"

He had found my website and glanced over one of my articles the day before. "You're great. That picture is so cute." He squeezed my arm. "Can't believe I'm telling you all of this. You're so easy to talk to."

"*Cute?*" I wanted to be as cute as the Statue of Liberty or the Mona Lisa…as cute as a mountain goat scrambling up the side of a craggy cliff.

"I should take you to Vegas. Bellagio. Drinks by the pool… It will be so hot." He squeezed my arm again.

"So I hear." I smiled noncommittally.

"No," he laughed, squeezing, yet again. "Vegas. You should come. You'd look so hot by the pool." He looked at the trail ahead. The incline was fairly steep. "Wanna walk back?"

He was a good kisser, and I hadn't locked lips in a while. But I found myself steadily pulling back. He was a sweet man and wanted to build into my life. But his construction materials were the accoutrements that filled physical space— not compartments in my brain. The adoration was gratifying, but non-nutritive. Our exchanges felt more like snacks than real conversations.

"I feel really close to you. We really have a connection don't we?"

He was sincere. I hungered for more.

Silent Sufferers

"It's fine." "Whatever you want." "Um sure. That's OK…" Pout. Shoulder slump. Weak smile.

Defining this guy's feelings and opinions will feel like holding soft gelatin. Pliability is terrific when molding clay, but too much softness in a grown man will erode respect. Quickly.

You can ask. But you can't make him answer.

There will be an urge to push at him, to find out what he really thinks and feels. But if he isn't comfortable with himself and/or is overly smitten with you, his feelings and opinions will only mirror yours. This isn't a comfortable situation for anyone.

He's hoping you'll notice, perceive or decipher. You will probably fail, however, because this guy is all about not sending any noticeable signals. That blip of an opinion may go off when your back is turned.

Do you really have time for this?

And "passive" can easily twist into insidious "passive-aggressive" communication—a silent and invisible war of wills. At the end of such a relationship, you may be left feeling you didn't know him at all. He didn't really reveal anything more than what he thought you might like to have across the dinner table.

Don't blame him. His comfort zone is small. But don't pursue and enable a partial connection like this. If you can't draw him out? Cut him out.

From the Field: *"Decaffeinated Drama"*

Jet lag was a factor. Had to be. No one muscles through twenty-five awake hours, two airline meals and six time zones without consequence.

So, when we awoke in Barcelona after a full day of travel and on-foot exploration of the Gothic quarter, my boyfriend and I needed some caffeine. A few more hours of sleep might have helped, but there was too much to see and do, so he ran out for coffee while I slo-mo'd my way towards launch.

He brought back two skinny paper cups of latte. "This is what they had," he shrugged, handing me one with a tiny tube of sugar.

"Thanks." I grabbed it, poured in the sugar and sipped happily as I rubbed sunscreen onto my shoulders and dug out a pair of flat-heeled sandals. I carried my paper cup into the tiny bathroom and inhaled more caffeine as I applied mascara. Finally, draining the cup, I brushed my teeth and swiped on some lip-gloss. The coffee had soothed my dull headache, and I felt almost perky as I grabbed sunglasses, my camera bag and our map. "Ready?"

He still seemed lethargic—my boyfriend. He hadn't

slept much on the plane.

"Breakfast?" he asked.

"Yeah. We need to eat."

"And we should grab lunch stuff," he added. "That place with the pesto cheese is around here somewhere."

I nodded. We had planned to picnic at Parc Guell, Antoni Gaudi's fanciful melding of nature and art. During our wander back to the hotel the previous night, we'd stumbled upon a specialty grocery with perfect picnic food.

"I think it's up here." I gestured ahead as we walked the avenue moments later.

"You think?"

"Yeah. It was by that corner place, right?" We were bleary from lack of sleep. He either knew exactly what I meant because we'd been together long enough for mind melding— or had no comprehension at all. The head nod he gave me could have meant either. If I'd paused, I might have noticed a frown. But I was busy following the map.

"It's this way," I pointed.

"The grocery?"

"No. Parc Guell. I think the grocery is on the way."

We walked on. The caffeine was carrying me, but I needed food too.

We covered a couple more blocks, peeking into groceries and cafes along the way. I knew he wanted the green pesto cheese and was determined to find it for him. "It has to be close!" I squinted down a side street.

"We missed it," he said glumly. "It was back there."

"What?"

"It was down the street where we got the sushi last night."

"Isn't that place up here?"

"No!"

I jumped. He was angry.

"It was back there! And we missed it. All I wanted was the green cheese!"

"Why didn't you say something?"

"You started walking!"

"But why didn't you just say you wanted the green cheese? We can still go back..."

"And you drank my coffee!"

"Huh?"

"You drank both of our coffees. When you were walking around getting ready, you picked up my coffee. You drank it. I didn't get any coffee."

Why didn't you tell me? "I'm sorry..."

CHAPTER SIX

DATING DECISIONS &
THE BENDABLE RULES

THE UNBENDABLE RULES are the ethical choices we'll discuss in Chapter Eleven. Deciding to follow the principles outlined below will likely make your dating life easier, but there will be exceptions. At the very least, give these concepts careful consideration before deciding to deviate from any of them.

Two-Years "Hands-Free"

It's one of my first questions when meeting a prospective date—after my standard soul-searcher, *"Will this be worth the lip gloss?"*—"How long have you been divorced?" Because I avoid dating anyone who isn't two years past the *"who gets the TVs/ children/friends"* personal-sized hurricane that divorce wreaks upon a life.

Why? Some personal experience, as well as the "can't

believe I did that" revelations from some of my single friends.

"Rule" sounds so unromantic. *But what if we click on every level? How can I not build a relationship with him?* And yes, occasionally—in a blue moon, in an alternate solar system, in another dimension—events may eclipse this one. But read on for some items to consider beforehand.

He needs to heal first. Divorce is trauma. Recovery takes time. Steps to healing include grief, acceptance and a massive rebuilding process. The reconstruction should include more than simply building a new life. Without some personal evaluation and growth, the newly single will fall into the same negative relational ruts.

Aren't you looking for more than "Train Wreck 2?"

Divorce is the public parade of two broken people. Almost always, there is a history of dysfunction and accommodation. There are obvious communication issues. Adultery, alcohol/ drug abuse, financial problems… Dysfunction is drawn to dysfunction. Unless the newly divorced corrects his part of the dysfunction equation, he will "fit" with a woman dysfunctionally similar to the wife he just escaped.

Is this really who you want to be?

Think about it. Establishing a new residence, adjusting parenting schedules, developing a personal life…these take time. It's hard. After six years, I'm *still* struggling to get the garbage out on trash day. Recreational dating is an easy distraction—the pursuit of another person is simple compared to fixing the one standing in your own gym shoes. It's tempting to use dating as an escape from the essential and more difficult mental work required to truly prepare for a healthy relationship.

What are you looking for? Casual entertainment or a long-term love?

Would I *ever* date a guy within my two-year window?

"Never" is a fairly random limitation. However, before allowing access to my heart, I would check to see if he bears any resemblance to the men I categorically avoid. A "perfect for me" guy at the wrong time of his life will *still* be unable to provide his steady half to the intimate stable grownup relationship we all desire. Hot, witty and handsome? Well… OK. I might take his number; mark the two-year anniversary of his new single life on my calendar and check back to see if he still wants coffee.

Avoid Office Romances

Yes, your male co-worker may be the only adult male you speak with besides the 20-something passing you lattes at the Starbucks drive-thru window—"*Here's your extra napkin, Ma'am,*" but be very cautious about venturing into an office romance. The risks are great.

The temptation is understandable. You've seen him at his best, cleanly shaven and showered. You're pretty sure his mom isn't dropping him off for work in the morning; you've observed him interacting with others and he smells pretty good in the elevator.

If it works out, you gain a carpool buddy, a mate who is more likely to understand the demands of your job and the opportunity to better coordinate scheduling.

However… if it ends, it could end badly. The worst of these breakups end up in headlines and courtrooms. But the less public endings can be equally painful and damaging. An ex in the office will no longer behave like the boyfriend he once was or even like the co-worker he still is—he's a hybrid and his behavior will be unpredictable. The two of you may do just fine as exes in the office, but you're rolling the dice, much like a mother carting a hungry toddler past the candy bars at checkout.

And if he breaks up with *you*, working with the man will

impact your ability to heal. There will be no buffer. Your home will hold memories; your office will hold him and pictures of his new girlfriend.

Think long and hard about this one. There are seven billion people on this planet. Is he really "that guy" or just the most convenient one available at the moment? There are many ways to extend your dating options that will be covered in Chapter Ten.

Yes, it's hard to argue against one of those rare "clicks," but take it slow. Double-check office rules and your own emotional stability. Are you ready for this? No whims in the workplace.

Multiple Marriages

Divorce is ugly. On the marriage report card, it's a solid F with snide "doesn't play well with others" comments scribbled into the margin. Happily married couples often don't get it. I certainly didn't understand the complexities of such a relational crash until undergoing my own grueling and heart-wrenching divorce.

These public breakdowns have many faulty components. The immediately obvious affair or alcohol issue may be a side effect of marital abuse or neglect. All of this may be tied to garbage that never got hauled to the curb after childhood.

So therapy really isn't an optional detour. It's the most direct route forward after a divorce. Each party needs to have a clear understanding of what happened in order to avoid a repeat. It wasn't his habit of throwing dirty clothes around the bedroom. And it wasn't that she quit wanting to have sex. These were just manifestations of underlying faulty conditions.

I give us each a mulligan—but only if we then buckle down and work on our game.

When I meet someone who has undergone more than one divorce—*"I basically married my ex-wife again"*—I hesitate. They may prove to be a terrific friend, but unless and until they are able to address whatever underlying issues have allowed them to repeat their intimacy disconnect, they represent a high-risk relationship to me.

My rule is not to date anyone with more than one divorce on his record. Again, this is a bendable rule, but only if a guy has done significant work to pinpoint his contribution to the marital failures and determined how he plans to avoid hitting "repeat."

Social Media Etiquette

Nowadays there's a quick exchange of business cards or digital share of contact info rather than a scrawled phone number on a slightly used napkin. And if he misplaces your card, he'll find you on Facebook.

You're on Facebook and LinkedIn, right?

"I don't do Facebook or Twitter." Many people have valid reasons for not participating in social media—privacy concerns, lack of time, inexperience—but without such a presence, you go from being "hard to get" to just plain "hard to find."

At minimum, put up a basic profile on Facebook and LinkedIn. It's part of the larger network strategy we'll be talking about in Chapter Ten. Adjust your privacy settings to your comfort level, but basically, this is your phonebook listing—*although I don't advise posting an actual phone number*. Put yourself where people can find you.

Now the more delicate matter is the "when to friend" question...

Facebook is my virtual Rolodex. If I want to maintain a

link or grow a friendship, I connect or hit "Add Friend" when I get the request. If there is potential romantic interest and other avenues of connection remain open, I wait on initiating any request. Maybe that's a leftover manifestation of the "don't call boys" rule of my youth, but I think it's valid. If you decide to initiate a virtual connection, pick one and only one. Barraging a guy with requests on Facebook, LinkedIn, Twitter, Foursquare, Instagram *and* Google looks as needy as the girl sending "Do you like me? Check 'Yes,' 'No' or 'Maybe'" notes in grade school.

If you are evaluating a potential date, a Facebook connection *will* give you a better sense of who that guy in the gym is away from the weight rack. *Note that I advocate an actual "friend" connection rather than spying.* Twitter, Instagram and Foursquare can give quick peeks at priorities and philosophies. But beyond basic verifications we discussed earlier, there's no need to "study up" on a date—TMI will leave you struggling to remember what you're "supposed" to know versus your snooped out discoveries. *You'll already have enough on your mind with getting the kids dropped off to dad on time and finding your date in the restaurant—keep the rest of it simple.*

Here's where it can get tricky: LinkedIn. This is a professional site, used for career and business connections. It's an excellent way to affirm professional credentials and gainful employment. If you have his first and last name or even a first name and a company or unique industry, it's usually worth the (anonymous—*sign yourself out, ladies!*) LinkedIn double-check.

But strive to keep those LinkedIn connections pure.

The great conundrum for "creatives" such as myself on LinkedIn is that virtually everyone is a potential client. And as a nationally published writer and columnist, as well as a voiceover/video personality, it isn't uncommon to receive connection requests from strangers in adjunct fields or business owners in need of my communication services. Filtering can be tricky for *all* of us. And if you're a committed connector as I am, one also needs to consider the possibilities of creating avenues for others and mentoring newbies.

However… Call me crazy, but CPAs and IT guys in other states? Medical personnel in other countries? Once upon a time Match.com meet-and-greets and old boyfriends? If there's mention of an article, business venture or shared contact, I'm receptive, but I've received more than a few questionable connection requests and have heard plenty of similar scenarios from my female friends.

My point is to *absolutely* include LinkedIn as part of your total networking strategy, but reserve it as a *reference tool only* when it comes to your social life. Don't become part of the problem by chasing down handsome photos—*that rarely display that ever-important ring finger anyway…*

But ignore social media altogether? That's the equivalent of the old unlisted phone number.

Watch Out for Whirlwinds

Being swept off one's feet plays better on the big screen than in your own neighborhood. My friend Danielle has been "swept" so many times, you'd think she was a dust bunny. I hate to disillusion her, but as her friend, I have to express my skepticism.

"This is different. It just feels 'right.'"

"Please tell me you haven't slept with him yet."

Silence.

The guy who falls in love in five minutes tends to be a flash-in-the-pan Bottom Dweller if the woman reciprocates or a Cling Wrap guy if she doesn't. I tend to attract Cling Wrap; Danielle attracts the leeches.

She's ready to fall in love and is a prime and rather pliable target—*and no, I'm not giving out her number to any gentleman readers.* Real romance is wonderfully thrilling, but I tend to wonder about a guy or gal who immediately has days at a time available for a new love. What happened to the rest of his or her life? To date, *none* of Danielle's whirlwinds have lasted a month. Once physical intimacy is breached, the whirlwind dies down, leaving Danielle to wonder what the hell just happened as she plants her feet and starts over again.

From the Field: *"LinkedIn, Love On"*

She giggled breathlessly, "You'll never believe who I heard from on LinkedIn... Rick!"

"The Cincinnati guy?"

"Yeah, well he explained all of that. He was in a really bad place. He says he can't stop thinking about me and wants to talk!"

My silence lacked enthusiasm, so Danielle elaborated on her good fortune.

"He's already sent me three emails this morning and wants to talk tonight. Of course, I'm cautious after what happened before, but he really seems to be doing better now!"

"What happened before" was that Danielle raced to spend a weekend "getting to know" Rick after a wild week of impassioned, soul-baring emails and phone calls. But their intense romantic weekend in a downtown hotel ended late that Sunday morning when he abruptly disengaged to get a jump on his workweek. He peeled out of the parking lot first, without a peek to the rearview mirror or a wave goodbye.

He disappeared.

Danielle felt betrayed. Stupid. Used...

"Be careful."

Danielle giggled again. "Of course. But he can't stop thinking about me, Heather. Isn't that crazy?"

Yep.

With Danielle fully engaged again, Rick accelerated quickly. Within a week, he was in town "on business." Danielle met him at his hotel. When he had meetings in another city an hour away the following week, Danielle met him there. She then drove across state lines for an overnight at his home in Kentucky.

A familiar pattern emerged.

Finally, she called, "I don't know." Her voice was flat.

"What do you mean? Rick?"

"Yeah. The weekend was amazing. But now I haven't heard from him in two days. I know he was out with friends last night, but he could have texted, don't you think? I'm free this next weekend. He knows that but hasn't tried to plan anything. Do I offer to drive down there again?"

"No. Let him come to you this time, Danielle. Or maybe you just need to step back entirely. He isn't being very respectful of your feelings."

"No. He's just adjusting, I think. It's been intense. Surprised us both. Maybe he's unsure of it all though. Too much too fast…"

"Maybe…"

"I think I'll call him. And just let him know that I could drive down Friday afternoon."

"Danielle, I wouldn't do that. Let it rest."

She called me again later that night. "He didn't respond."

"You called?"

"Texted. Said I could bring some work down with me and be available Friday evening. He hasn't responded."

Danielle and Rick cycled through three more weeks. After each bout of intense intimacy, he would retreat with a "do not disturb" aura trailing his exit. Danielle agonized between running after him and turning away from the toxic situation. Eventually, her sense of self-preservation kicked in and the relationship skidded to an emotionally charged, rather venomous conclusion.

In the end, Danielle's dalliance with Rick was less of a whirlwind than a havoc-wreaking straight-line wind.

No Sex Before Six

When it comes to physical intimacy, the longer you wait and the more hours you spend getting to know someone first, the better. And the longer *he* is willing to wait, the more likely it is that he is truly interested in *you*, and not just the female gender in general.

Build respect by pacing the relationship.

Men and women in their second single lives are usually clear on how everything works physically and on what attracts them. That isn't the issue. Physical intimacy too soon will stunt a potentially good relationship. In worst cases it will generate feelings of closeness to a virtual stranger who never calls his kids and is behind on his mortgage payments—and extrication will be difficult, because you've already been sucked in by his amazing bedroom tricks.

Some women use sex to fall in love, and it's well known that the chemicals released with orgasm—oxytocin and vasopressin—act to heighten our feelings of attachment and trust. So if you want to "be in love," sex can help you get there. However, if you want to be in love with the right guy, let your brain and heart lead the way. If you're an adult woman seeking a long-term relationship, you will have better success if sex is a decision—not a side effect of too much alcohol and a long cold winter.

The first date or meet-and-greet is for talking and arm touching and maybe, hopefully, a hug. If you wonder what it would be like to kiss him—go on a second date to find out. Third dates are the breakout point. *I don't have many third dates.*

Wait at *least* six dates for actual "by *anyone's* definition" sex—and space those meetings out a little. Fit in some phone conversations and the stuff of daily life. Give yourself time to figure out if it's just an attraction or if you really do enjoy his company and conversation. Few of us can truly relegate sex to a purely physical act, but those aforementioned chemicals are a powerful lure. Six dates won't always be enough, but with our busy schedules it will ensure a reasonable passage of time between that first kiss and naked gymnastics.

There have been guys to whom I experienced a high initial attraction that I never slept with because the rest of it—his values, where he was in life—just didn't line up, and the attraction faded. Some friends consider that a wasted opportunity; others recognize that avoiding physical intimacy where emotional intimacy will not be possible as a real time-saver.

We aren't kids anymore. We're intelligent passionate adults. I still like to play with fire, but I'm going to choose when to light that match.

Avert "Drift"

Without consistent communication and face-to-face time, "drift" happens. Symptoms: You kind of start to forget one another's schedule. Maybe you let his calls roll to voicemail. Any actual conversations get generic (and are accompanied by the faint sound of keyboard tapping)—"*Good. How about you?*"

Drift is death to relationships.

In an exclusive dating relationship, at minimum, aim for once-a-day phone calls, that cover more than the weather, and twice-a-week dates. Minimum. Anything less than that kind of commitment says that one—or both—of you really isn't interested in growing the relationship. Obviously, travel and the occasional crisis can intrude on the schedules of two gainfully employed adults, but remaining connected is a choice. Recognize that a long-term relationship lacking in true emotional intimacy is essentially a long-term pause on your journey to finding the "right guy." It will be obvious if one of you hasn't made connection a priority, and the next logical choice might be to complete the disconnect.

Friends First; Kids Last

If you think this might be the guy you'll take to your class reunion in five years? See what your friends and adult family members think. If the thought of bringing him along to your favorite hangouts makes you uncomfortable, you'd better figure out why. These worlds must merge or you'll find yourself spinning in alternate orbits, losing contact with essential parts of the life you've built. By that fifth or sixth date, it's time to bump into friends while you're out with the new guy. Don't force it, but don't forgo it either.

But spare your younger kids the *Almost* men (coming up in Chapter Seven). There's simply no need—or excuse—to put them through a bunch of first meetings with men you're still evaluating. Be a parent first. Yes, squeezing your dating life into the spaces devoid of children will slow the pace of getting to know a new guy, but chances are he'll respect you for that decision (and possibly be alarmed if introduced to your kids too quickly). Wait until you're fairly confident your new man will be around for the next holiday before arranging low-key introductions with the younger set.

Caveat: My kids are older and know that my circle includes many platonic male friends. They've met some of these guys because I think it's important they learn to value the opposite gender as individual people first and dating material second. But still, they never meet a guy I deem a potential romantic connection unless I've stepped over that demarcation line into active relationship building.

From The Field: "*Pool Party*"

The weeds were winning the lawn war, but I'd preemptively closed the doors on two messy kids' bedrooms and was burned out on all things house-related. Lou had a charismatic smile. And he kissed like he knew what came next...

He had charmed me over flatbread and the house cabernet at my favorite Italian restaurant. And had fueled my interest over cold beer in a completely dead dive bar with a little strategic under the table foot action. Call it chemistry, but I drove the twenty minutes to join him at his summer pool of choice without complaint when he asked.

"You free on Saturday? You should join us at the pool! I'll rub sunscreen anywhere you need it..."

"Us?"

"Yeah. Me and the kids."

Yep, it seemed odd that he wanted me to interact with his

two kids before he had fully vetted me. But I knew myself to be great with kids, and this had happened before. A woman's lack of obvious flaws is "good enough" for many lonely men juggling shared parenting. Basic normal social skills made me "kid worthy."

"Hi!" He met me at the entrance with an electric smile.

I pulled on the lower edge of my tank top to bring it down over the upper edge of my wrap skirt. *Sequester the abs. His kids are here.*

"Hey!" I smiled, trying to avoid a verbal fumble. The bathing suit date was a new and slightly awkward concept for me. I was ready to jump into the water and present a bare-skinned face, but I wavered on shedding the necessary layers of clothing to get there. I didn't own a one piece and had selected a turquoise bikini solely for the relative strength of its elastic.

"Wow, you look great."

He lightly touched my arm and started a tingle that made me blush. "Mmm… Need some sunscreen on those shoulders?"

"I do… Think you could handle that?"

"I think I could handle a lot of things."

We edged around the pool, dodging a cannonball splash. My eyes scanned the packed poolside pavement for child eyes aimed in our direction. "Where are your kids?"

"Oh they're over there by the slide." He motioned and then waved, his hand quickly slipping off of the small of my back. I followed his gaze and saw a hand in the air. "That's Sam. I told them to wait on the chairs until I brought you back."

"And remind me of your daughter's name?"

"Anna."

"Oh yeah… Right."

Moments later, Sam and Anna greeted me with mild curiosity.

"Kids, this is Miss Heather."

They muttered polite hellos.

"So, how old are you guys?"

"12," said Sam.

"10." Anna glanced at the water. "Can we get back in the pool now?"

Lou's grin had serious wattage. "Sure honey. But let's get a little more sunscreen on first."

Once he had rubbed some lotion onto his daughter's shoulders, he turned to me. "Need some on *your* back?"

I eyed his daughter. "I can probably get it myself, but thanks."

Lou caught on. "You two go ahead—shallow end—and we'll join you in just a minute."

Sam looked doubtful. "You're going to get in the water, aren't you?"

"Of course!" Lou beamed at him and then waved them both off. "Scoot you two. We'll be there in a minute."

I gave him my back, and he massaged SPF30 into my skin like flavored body oil. "How are your legs?"

"Better not in front of your kids…"

"They aren't going to see," he wheedled.

I shook my head with a smile. "Huh uh. You'll have to work your way down to leg application, I'm afraid."

He fake pouted and then relaxed into another grin.

"I'm glad you came. We're here every Saturday. This is our regular spot." He motioned toward a cooler, "Need anything to eat? Drink?"

"No thanks. I'm good."

"I bet you are."

Smile. "Your shoulders are a little red. Want me to hit them?" I nodded at the tube of sunscreen he was slipping into a duffle bag.

"Nah. I don't believe in sunscreen. I don't really burn." He nodded toward his reddened skin. "This'll tan over by tomorrow."

"Daddy, aren't you coming?" Sam and Anna stood dripping at the foot of our chaises: Anna hunched forward, arms crossing her chest with a shiver and Sam standing tall and squinting against the sun.

"Yup! We were just heading over." Lou reached for my hand and pulled me from the chair. I sucked in my stomach and whipped off my outerwear with the same close-your-mind discipline that helped me dive into icy pools for 8am swim lessons in fifth grade. Lou did a strategic "ladies first" and followed me to the pool's edge. I could feel his eyes on my turquoise butt and resisted the urge to repeatedly adjust the bikini bottom.

"Marco Polo, Daddy?" Anna asked, her eyes lighting up when Lou met her gaze.

"Sure!"

We played the game until rest period came ten minutes later.

Lou and I did some adult swim time while the kids munched on carrots and pretzel rods. Mostly, we stood in the water pretending we weren't aware of the meager inches between our bodies.

"So, what's your week like? Want to grab another beer?"

"Um, I need to check. Officially, I'm free on Tuesday and Wednesday nights, but Matt wants to hang on one of those."

Lou smiled hopefully. "Well, let me know. You could

come over and sample some of my grilled chicken either night. It's a family favorite!"

I spent a few minutes talking with Anna before the whistle released the under-eighteens back to the chlorinated water. "Art, I guess."

I'd asked about her favorite classes. She was quieter than Sam.

The afternoon passed quickly. I planned to meet friends at 6 and needed to fit in a run first. It was time to leave.

Lou had the kids sit on the chairs again while he walked me to my car. He hopped a little on the pavement, having left his flip-flops by the chaises. Still, he leaned in for a long, lingering kiss.

His lips were soft, and my insides melted.

"Tuesday…?" he asked.

"If I can…"

He dipped his head to kiss my shoulder and then pulled me closer.

I felt his attraction. And my own.

"We have something here. You feel it, right?"

I nodded. Smiled. And felt awkward for him: Mr. Mom shifting into a Would-be-Lover. Back and forth and back again. A whistle blew in the background.

"Sounds like rest period's over."

"They'll wait on the chairs like I told them."

But they shouldn't have to… Not yet…

The Texting Trap

Texting is like talking with a mouthful of peanut butter. Words and intentions are misunderstood. It can be a passive-aggressive minefield of spurts and long silences. Conflicts can be deliberately avoided—or conversely, created. Texting allows us to multi-task instead of focusing on connecting with an individual person.

One thing my failed relationships have in common was increased texting towards their conclusions. We had lost that burning desire to share things verbally. I even let calls roll to voicemail and texted my responses.

Now, I can be a rather witty texter. I enjoy keeping in touch with a favorite guy—and friends/kids—via texting when I'm unable to have a conversation. The critical difference lies in choosing to text rather than talk. In my romantic relationships, this was a red flag I should have noticed.

If you are serious about building a strong relationship—no texting, if you can talk instead. Grownups aim for direct face-to-face communication in their romantic relationships.

Crisis Creation

After a few relationships, we start to recognize patterns. He doesn't call when he said he would, and it reminds you of how your ex ignored you for the last eight years of marriage. He says he has to leave early on Sunday to get started on some things for the workweek, and you remember how ex-boyfriend Jim used to spend his Saturdays vacuuming his condo instead of getting together as planned.

We interpret silences and sentences, reading in meanings that simply aren't there—using lazy and protective thinking that will get in the way of honest understanding.

Him: "Wanna just watch a movie tonight?"

Her: *Oh god. He's flipping on the TV. He doesn't want to talk anymore.*

Him: *She doesn't like this one?*

Her: *He's flipping channels. He's already bored with me* (She's already figuring out how to describe this to her friends to get an interpretation of her interpretation)!

Asking is easier. "Everything OK? You didn't call last night." or "Do you need some space? Want to talk about it?" Separate yourself from the situation a little. It isn't always about you. Most of the time, it will be about them. So don't swirl into a panic and create a problem that isn't there. Leave the drama to the professionals on stage and screen.

Your Personal Deal Breakers

A: "I'm just not ready to raise another man's children. Raising my own was rewarding enough, thank you!"

B: "I can't date someone lacking a world-view. He has to be aware of the bigger picture beyond our city, state and country."

C: "I really take care of myself. Is it too much to expect the guy I date to work out occasionally?"

D: "I'm allergic to cats."

I've heard each of these defined "deal breakers" from the mouths of friends. So when A talks about the attractiveness of a busy dad or D dives into a relationship with tissues and box of Benadryl... well, love—or even the hope of love—can enable new levels of tolerance, I guess... But, be sure you're truly tolerant and not silently fuming that your new love won't send his kids to the ex-wife on the weekend or that Fluffy is permitted to sleep on the bed.

When you buy a house, you may be able to compromise

on the neighborhood or size of the yard. You may be willing to overlook dingy carpeting because flooring is replaceable. But there will be homes you won't even drive by because they lack a garage or a bathroom or are simply out of your price range, right?

Keep an open mind, but know thyself. Fluffy could have kittens and then where would you be?

What must you have? What must you not have? Eye color had better not be on this list. Marital status and a few personal values had better be near the top. Be honest with yourself and make some decisions ahead of time—it's hard to be rational with soft jazz playing in the background. Reevaluate as you go—a big part of dating is learning about who *you* really are, and self-discovery may impact your list of relationship essentials.

Chapter Seven

~

Are We There Yet?

ALMOST can work for a while, but it has a definite shelf life. Let's define what *Almost* isn't, and then, what it is.

Almost is not necessarily a man who has revealed a flaw, a weakness or demonstrated that he can be momentarily distracted.

You have flaws, weaknesses and distractions too.

Almost is *not* necessarily the guy who is having a temporary "hard time" with his kids or job. If he's making efforts to resolve an issue, even seeking a therapist to help himself be a better parent or person—it might be worth sticking around to see who he becomes.

Men are not moved into the *Almost* category during adjustment periods in which the two of you are figuring out schedules and needs and how to be a couple—because relationship building is hard! It takes time, and there will be misunderstandings along the way. You can't allow fears or miscommunication to send you toward the exit prematurely.

When I was learning to ride a two-wheeler, I developed a habit of leaping off my bike at the first wobble. My self-preservation instinct was so extreme that my bike never got a scratch. I had time to jump off, land on two feet and catch it before it ever hit the pavement. *Circling the block took me longer than the average kid.*

Past experiences can lead many of us to "leap" out of a relationship the first moment we feel ignored, disregarded or insulted. Fear prevents questions and real communication. We move on to the next candidate and wait for him to make a similar mistake, circling potential relationships like a timid kid on a wobbly bike.

Beware of looking for excuses to quit on a new relationship that might be worth an investment of time and committed communication. Walls of self-protection can shield us from *both* heroes and villains.

On the other hand, *Almost* **is** the really great successful guy whom everyone loves but who is kind of boring to be with alone. You find yourself reaching for the TV remote whenever you sit down together. Evenings are noticeably better with wine and outside entertainment.

Almost **is** the man who was recently divorced (or broke up with a long-term girlfriend) and simply isn't ready for another relationship yet. You keep thinking that in another week, he'll recognize how wonderful you are and be ready to focus and plan and be a real couple—but next week always leads to another week and a lot of wondering.

Almost **is** the guy who is still angry with his ex. You're pretty sure he loves you, but he's still focused on the battlefield behind him. He doesn't even like her, but he can't seem to extricate her from his thoughts and conversations.

Almost may even be the guy you're with while you're still wondering if your ex is thinking about you. *Not often. And certainly not all the time. Just now and then. And then, Now, again...*

Almost will feel like tending a seed that sprouts a shoot but never matures enough to yield any real fruit.

Grownups keep growing.

From the Field: *"Handfuls of Maybes"*

We were comparing men to fresh green beans and discussing the importance of the selection process last night.

Yes, there was wine on the table.

What we were really talking about, however, was our common desire to avoid regrets and our common *mistake* of grabbing handfuls of "maybes" as if there would never *ever* be another option before us.

My fellow wine sippers are kind, smart, attractive women. But we've lingered in relationships that didn't work. From time to time, we've waited on improvements in adjoining areas of our lives when we should have been decisive. We've settled for "good" when we should have held out for "good fit."

"You went flat. I could see it on your face and hear it in your voice. He was totally wrong for you."

I nodded. She was right.

But we weren't doing Happy Hour analysis on me. She was the one who, after a bike wreck and bad Percocet moment, had reneged on our signed and dated agreement to abstain from a grueling and emotionally draining relationship.

"You went back and forth with him for five years!" She nodded and winced. I wanted to say, "At least you didn't marry him." But she had...

It was a mirrored mistake: propping up unhealthy relationships, romantic and otherwise. Making emotional investments with too high an expense ratio. Whether due to bad timing, mismatched priorities or overblown optimism: these "good people" hadn't been good for *us*. At least, not in the capacity we'd permitted them into our heads or beds.

This is where the green beans strung into the conversation, not surprisingly, timed to our second glasses of wine.

"We're afraid," I pronounced. "We're so afraid of throwing away something 'good' that we clutch that first handful without really examining what we're holding. Instead of being truly selective—*'Nice green bean for someone else'*—we stop simply because 'it's green' and 'it's a bean!'"

"Just think of the time we've wasted in mediocre places, when we live in such a big world..." I looked at Percocet Girl. "You were focused on downsizing yourself to fit into a relationship that had the same issues at the end as it did at the beginning."

"Me too," I added.

"We're good at nurturing and accepting," Friend Two said.

"Which is good, but I don't *need* another fixer-upper!"

Percocet Girl nodded. "We're afraid of losing little things."

"Which distracts from the big things."

"We have to trust ourselves," Friend Two said.

"And have good backup."

Clink.

Respect Required

This is a four-way stop. It *has* to be for the relationship to work in the long-term. Here's how it works: He respects you. He respects himself. You respect yourself. You respect him.

If any of these are missing there will be a collision, and someone will get hurt.

Signs of respect include: allowing one another to make individual decisions, disclosing these decisions to one another, being open to one another's input and sharing joint decisions.

Sounds a lot like basic communication, and yes, focused consistent communication is one of the biggest indicators of respect.

Respect also includes consideration and some accommodation of differences. Your way of approaching a problem—or even dinner preparation—may be very different than his. One isn't necessarily better than the other. What is essential, however, is that there is a healthy balance to your joint choices.

If he always does things your way—one (or both) of you doesn't respect him. And if you feel uncomfortable mentioning that you'd really prefer sushi to pizza...or that you'd like to hang out with your friends instead of his for a change? Something is out of alignment at that four-way stop.

Bending and Blending

If you have children, it's advisable to shield them from your fledgling dating life. They're already dealing with a major life change, and watching you teeter on high heels to greet a stranger at the front door is too much too soon.

But over time, if you plan on building anything real with a man, you will have to eventually bring him into the world that includes your family and friends. Sure it's easier to keep him over *there*, relegated to Tuesday nights. No stress beyond choosing your dress. No worrying if your friends will find him pleasantly quirky or just odd. No concerns as to whether he can cheer at the appropriate moments at your kid's soccer games. But if you're serious about making a life with a man, he gets to be part of the life you already have.

That was always my glitch. For the first few years after my divorce, I maintained two lives. I was Mom when the kids were with me, and Heather when they were at their dad's. It seemed complicated, and I guess it was. Even when their dad was steadily dating the woman who is now his wife, I remained "Mom," unwilling to bring anyone new into our little family group. Oh, I dated. But they were phantom men. I dated one guy for two years, and he only met my kids once. By accident.

I lacked confidence in both my choices and in myself, and so the two worlds remained separate. Protective? Maybe. Cowardly? Absolutely.

But also, I'd simply chosen the wrong guys—men that I couldn't fathom blending into the life I had built. They were relegated to Tuesdays because I was unwilling to include them at a band concert or family hiking day.

This essentially doomed those relationships. It became obvious that while I was happy to be part of the worlds of these men, I wouldn't allow them into mine. They became *Almost* men.

If you can't envision a blending, this is not a long-term relationship.

If I can't imagine him joining me at a cross-country meet, he has no place in my romantic life.

From the Field: *"Gutter Balls"*

I blamed it on a need to simplify. Bringing anyone new into my precarious "triple teenager" home life seemed unnecessarily bold and hormonally hazardous.

"Saturday won't work. I have my kids."

He nodded quickly, knowing better than to reorganize my thoughts on the matter.

"But Tuesday? At my place?"

"Sure!" And yes, I was more than willing to spend time with him and his pre-teen boys. Sometimes, the best part of hanging out with Tim was admiring Chris' artwork or Aaron's latest Lego creation.

We tried blending our families on a Sunday afternoon after my kids had finally met Tim. I could only convince my youngest son Matt to accompany me to the bowling alley, however. My oldest was firmly entrenched in his first year of college, and my daughter, when presented with the alternate universe available at her dad's, opted for Pluto.

"Why do I have to go when Hannah doesn't?"

I had no good answer except, "C'mon. It'll be fun!"

Once we'd navigated shoe and ball selection, the boys sat obediently, waiting their turns on the lane. Had they been classmates, they would have opted for different lunch tables in the cafeteria. I couldn't see them ringing one another's doorbell for a pickup football game either. Actually, I wasn't sure Tim's boys would even play. Every nerve in my body was aware of the silences and averted eyes. There was no "Wanna shoot hoops later?" or "Now, settle down you guys!" I perked up when Matt made a non-essential comment to Chris, but when Tim tried to keep it rolling; it fell flat on his effervescent effort.

It wasn't a bad afternoon, but we only *talked* about doing a repeat.

"Yeah, we really should get the boys together again…"

And I realized that the mountain before us was but a heavily foreshadowed foothill.

Tim came to dinner on one of Matt's nights with me. He struggled with video football but gamely played on with Matt. We brought out the Scrabble board over dinner. Tim tanked. Even worse—he looked nervous.

"It's not his thing," I explained the next morning. "But did you have fun playing the football game?"

Matt shrugged. "He never scored." He raised his eyebrows, and his small forced smile grew into a genuine grin. "He tried. Really hard. But he sucked, Mom. I got my all time scoring record!"

"Thanks for trying," I told him. While thinking that this was the conversation I should be having with Tim. Not my son.

We slowed down on sharing family space, Tim and I. There was a soccer game that spring. Two congruent games actually. His oldest son, Aaron, and Matt had games on adjoining fields at a neighborhood park. Tim and I joked via text messages about our proximity to one another amidst the shivering suburban parents and then I traded phone for camera, knowing I'd see him for dinner that evening. My ex, his fiancée and my daughter were ensconced in collapsible chairs with front row views—I wasn't about to parade to Aaron's field. Or ask Tim to join me.

But what I found to be a fun coincidence—"Ha ha, I *think* I see you! Field to the east, right?"—Tim processed as yet another diminishment of our relationship.

"It felt odd. You were right there. And I couldn't walk over and give you a hug."

"Well no. My kids were there!" *Did I really need to explain this any further?* "And the ex and his fiancée were there too, you know! Awkward!"

Tim shrugged. "Felt odd."

I figured we were done with the conversation because I'd punctuated and moved on, taking the only path available to me. But the conversation looped on for Tim. He felt like "less." And that mattered more and more.

Establishing Exclusivity

This is the demarcation line. Until the two of you agree to be exclusive to one another, you're only dating. Exclusivity makes you a true couple and that twice a week dinner thing you're doing a relationship. If you're aiming for the long-term, this understanding should come *before* physical intimacy.

No one really wants to risk rejection by bringing it up however, and if you've met through an online dating site, there's that delicate issue of his posted profile...

First, do *not* bring this up—or even worse, start "hinting" about it—prematurely. You may feel drawn to someone immediately, but aim for magnetism over being a refrigerator magnet. I'm not advocating game playing. What I'm suggesting is that you hold a little back. Don't hit him with your dysfunctional childhood and entire dating history on the first date. Don't beg for the details of his last relationship, first relationship and every woman in between. Pacing a relationship is very important in the beginning. Many women rashly leap on board before they even know what boat they're on. They itch to "define" a relationship—a topic that, when broached too soon, will translate roughly into "Welcome to prison. Hand over your life and all personal items."

And physical intimacy too soon will wreck that ship before it sails. *What? You won't know for sure until you sleep with him? Nonsense. You can get enough essential information on the chemistry question topside.*

So... You know he's the only guy you want on your calendar. You've hidden your online profile because phone calls from anyone else just make you miss his voice.

"Do I say something?? I think he still has his profile up!"

"How long have you been dating now?"

"Three weeks. Three times this week already! Eight or nine dates, I think. We haven't, you know, had a sleep-over or anything, but it's getting serious."

"Ask him."

"What??"

"If you're getting more physical, it's a reasonable question to ask. Just say, 'We're spending a lot of time together. I'd kind of like to see where this could go. Are you ready for that kind of step or do you still need to see other people for a while longer?"

"I can't do that! He might say he isn't ready or that he doesn't think I'm the one."

"But then you'd know."

And better to know something like that before things get "serious"—our euphemism for "sexual."

If the extra toothbrush has arrived and he still has a profile posted? I'd be sticking that toothbrush in with my cleaning supplies.

Holding Onto the Wrong Bird

You want to make it work. After the novelty of online dating wears off and you've swum a few fruitless laps in the dating pool, there may be a stronger-than-ever desire to sprint through the whole process.

While your married friends are reading romance novels next to snoring husbands, dreaming that *single* men simultaneously smolder, smooch and spout soulful phrases of endearment, you've learned that a lot of them have "unfinished business" and that the smolder may be indiscriminate—or simply an indication that dinner didn't sit well.

Dating takes energy, time and courage. The thought of settling into something—anything—*solid* can sound pretty appealing. While it takes time to discover if a relationship can and should work in the long-term and you have the ability to learn something valuable from any situation, not stepping away from an inherently flawed relationship simply because it's comfortable is a decision to miss other opportunities to grow and possibly find the relationship that *will* work.

From the Field: "*Wednesdays and Every Other Weekend*"

In retrospect, it was probably a terrific clue. As a writer with strong sleuthing skills, it's strange that I didn't pick up on it. Maybe I didn't want to know.

My friend Danielle noticed it immediately. "You're flat," she said, climbing onto the elliptical machine beside me at the gym. She wasn't talking about my compressing sports bra. "You aren't happy."

I argued. "Yes, I am. We're just more settled now. It's OK. It's good."

She stared me down. Danielle is one of those friends willing to sacrifice politeness for kindness. "It is *not*."

I waited, mentally generating and dismissing proofs that she was wrong.

"I've seen you walk in here with him." *Him*, being my boyfriend of almost two years, and *"I've seen"* including evidence she and I had discussed many times before. Yes, I'd taken the huge step of bringing him to my gym, but it had felt like a courtesy, not a "come, play in my world" kind of thing. Danielle had listened. Danielle had observed. She is a grafted "sister" on my family tree and, as such, had heard numerous explanations for this relationship that was, quite simply, a lot of work.

And still, I tried. After twenty-one months, give or take a break-up or two when burning lungs had sent me shooting to the surface for air, I was committed to both my path and my pain. "He is so kind to me. He loves me, Danielle. He's just a little needy sometimes. It's probably me…"

"Do you love *him*?" I noticed that she hadn't turned on her machine's TV screen. The sound was off on my own.

"Of course, I care about him! He's a good man!"

"That's not in question. He's very sweet," she grimaced, giving me no ground to play that card.

"You know him! He's a good guy!"

"He is," she slowed her pace to turn and meet my eyes. "That doesn't mean he's good for *you*."

I notched up my resistance level, sipped from my water bottle and asked about her day. That bought me about two deflecting sentences before she set in again.

"Heather, you're flat! I see it; I hear it…this isn't a good place for you."

13, 12, 11... I tapped my machine's resistance down to 10. "Danielle, I promised to make this work. I've put in almost two years. I'm getting older! I have to make this work! I quit on my marriage. I can't quit again!"

"You told me you're happy when he leaves."

"No! I didn't say that! Just that...well, I'm just relieved sometimes. I'm used to having some space, Danielle! I've... well, I've been canceling some of our Wednesday nights. He doesn't like that. But, we still have some windows every other weekend!"

She shrugged, knowing that I'd sort through our conversation later.

And I did. *When did "Wednesdays and every other weekend" become "Saturday, maybe...?"*

"You aren't into him." Danielle had tossed that phrase at me several times.

I guess I had taken that as a judgment on me, not an assessment of a situation...but "forever" suddenly sounded like extended confinement on a sunny afternoon.

And it's already Tuesday again...

It is always better to be alone by yourself, than alone with someone else.

The Disappearing Act

Don't do it. It isn't kind. Grownups don't pretend they missed a phone call or that they're just *really busy*. It wasn't nice in middle school, and now you know better, so there's really no excuse.

Grownups *own up*. Immediately. *Before* they start flirting with a guy at the office or checking out another girl at the gym.

Breaking off a relationship can be excruciating for both the sender and receiver of such a message. But a grownup participates in this, nonetheless, because clear communication erases confusing thoughts and allows the other person the opportunity to move on. He or she does *not* simply disappear no matter how long or short the connection might have been. Basic decency dictates that we communicate our intentions. Disappearing is cowardly. It's racing for the lifeboat without a thought to other passengers.

Many avoid giving a clear breakup message because it's uncomfortable. Maybe you did it badly in the past and fear a repeat.

"You'd think he'd get the message! I haven't returned any of his calls or anything!"

Well, no. Silence is not a clear message. It forces the other party to make guesses and possibly worry about your well-being.

Clean up your messes. A fellow human being is worth a five-minute phone call. If you can't manage the discomfort of delivering bad news, you simply aren't ready for a relationship. The couplehood you hope for will likely include occasional conflict. You should be able to say "no" in a kind way before you ever say "yes."

Sometimes we do want to do the right thing, but simply run a deficit on the appropriate phrasing. I'll give you some suggestions for specific scenarios in Chapter Eleven.

CHAPTER EIGHT

❧

HELPING YOURSELF & THE "RESET"

SOMETIMES YOU JUST have to hibernate. My friend Joe refers to it as "the bat cave." It's quiet. And kind of a dark place. But your best friends will still meet you there for coffee—stepping carefully over Life's guano—to keep you company and encourage you.

They may say things like, "You're a good guy; you just made a bad choice," or "I never liked him anyway." They will remind you of his grating laugh, frat boy humor and small shoe size (*wink*). Good friends will remind you of who you *really* are when you're wobbly with grief over a relationship that wasn't meant to be.

Joe and I met for coffee several times while he was dwelling in his bat cave and I was negotiating the lease on my own hibernation space. We sifted, sorted and looked for reasonable answers over buttered bagels. We affirmed our own good intentions. And it helped. A lot.

It helped even more to remove myself from dating for several months while I sorted through my pattern of choices that had left me working too hard for so little reward. Joe's bat cave sounded depressing, but even one more "go nowhere" date sounded even worse.

Eventually, I bee-lined my way to therapy. It felt like an emergency, and I guess it was. Towards the end of my first session after I'd listed my life traumas, I asked, "Is that a lot? 'Cause to *me*, it feels like a lot..." My therapist affirmed that it was indeed a hell of a lot, and I launched into several weeks of identification, redefinition and eventually a growth toward resilience.

Dating? Didn't have time for that. I was busy taking care of something more important. Me.

I needed dedicated time to grow myself into someone I'd enjoy hanging out with for the rest of my life. I needed a "reset."

It was an excellent choice. That pause was essential to solidifying both my boundaries and my expectations. If I'd merged into the dating stream prematurely, I could easily have shot off course with any strong inviting current, however ill advised. I first needed to chart my own course and simply wait on healing.

Sudden space in our lives, especially after the loss of a relationship, can be painfully uncomfortable. Removing reminders and purposefully creating new habits is critical. The old relationship, however unhealthy, created a comfortable rut in our lives. There's a strong tendency to slide into the same familiar pattern again with a similarly unhealthy relationship or to fill that vacuum with alcohol/drugs, overwork, over-exercise or "recreational dating." While a career or health focus can pay off if moderated, abusing alcohol and/or dating indiscriminately will simply glue you to the very spot you hate. You're setting your own trap from which to whine about the lack of "good men" and wonder why you can't seem to meet them. Better to step away, reassess and regroup—and that takes time. It takes long conversations with those who know you best and finding ways to fill your life that don't involve a rollercoaster ride through random dating.

When you're needy, you will accept less than you deserve. A reset allows you to grow your own strength rather than leech it from others. It enables you to make better choices. Afraid you're running out of time? *Have* to start dating *right now*? The truth is that you will save yourself considerable time and heartache by taking the weeks (or months) necessary to fill in empty spaces and establish your own relational goals *first*. Once dating is no longer a "need," but rather an accessory to your already fabulous life, you have permission to don those sexy shades and exit the bat cave. *But scrape off your shoes on the way out.*

Dignity-Be-Damned Desperate Choices

We're smarter than we think we are. It's only paranoia when we apply our reservations in a general fashion. Sometimes, we just have a "feeling." Or have a feeling that we *should* have a feeling...

Desperate choices are the ugly moments shared only with our closest friends—those whispered admissions that bond us with the realization of how low we can truly go and the turning points from which we pledge to hold one another to higher standards. These include my friend who slept with her married chiropractor after discovering her husband modeling business suits for another woman and my friend who reluctantly attended an adult sex party in an effort to keep a relationship afloat. Other "uglies": showing up for repeated late night booty calls with a completely uncommitted man, faithfully waiting for months on a fickle guy off on a "secret mission," sleeping with an ex-boyfriend's best friend, sleeping with a sister's ex-boyfriend, texted ultimatums, tearful voicemails... Every friend has a handful worth cringing over. It's an endless list—and the main reason I first began writing this book.

A desperate choice is compulsive, impulsive and almost always, incorrect. It's a futile attempt to ankle grab a departing love interest in hope of turning vapor to solid.

We make these kinds of decisions when we forget or willfully ignore our alternatives. These choices go with statements such as "I'm *not* going to be alone," "I can't *live* without him," "He *can't* live without me," and "That's the *last* time...!" And, these desperate choices usually *will* create a "last time" with the target, because they can be real bridge burners.

They can also be revelatory. Learning to trust in your strength to overcome life's challenges is empowering. Knowing that friends are available to help you do it? Even better.

From the Field: *"What's Your SAT Score?"*

I scanned the dark interior of the sports bar for my meet-and-greet guy, camouflaging nervousness with a smile and hoping I wouldn't run into a neighbor. *"Umm...No thanks, I'm meeting someone... Nooo, I don't see him yet. Actually, I'm not sure if I'll even recognize him..."* Awkward.

I had reluctantly re-upped for Match after Jim and I broke things off. Danielle pushed me to "get back out there," and I was doing my feeble best. Meet-and-greet Mack found me at a high top table when he walked in ten minutes late.

"Hey! You look nice."

Mack was slightly under my minimum age, but I was in a state of post breakup open-mindedness. *Older didn't work. Let's try "younger" this time.* We ordered beers.

"You're a writer?!" He was quite pleased. "My life is *really* interesting. You should write about *me*! I should honestly be your next book!"

He began fairly close to the beginning and ordered us second beers shortly after his varsity football career and high school graduation. I should have made a graceful exit but hadn't been out in weeks. And I had painted my nails—kind of a big deal for me.

Finally, he turned the conversation to me. "Hey, what's your SAT score?"

I smiled. "What?"

"Your SAT. What did you get on it? I got a 1450. Could have gone higher if I'd taken it again. What was yours?"

I kept smiling because I didn't know what else to do with my lips. "I have no idea. Don't really remember."

"Sure you do!" He grinned at me.

"No. I really don't." I regretted painting my nails.

From there he launched chronologically until the part where his fiancé's baby failed the paternity test he had requested. "I got the envelope at work. Walked out to a bar and got shit-faced. Broke off the engagement. Wasn't going to keep another guy's kid."

We floundered there for a moment.

"I'm sorry." *And I was. For his heartbreak. For the girl and the kid. For letting him order me a second beer...*

"You don't just lay a little wax paper over the food?"

"Nah. She always cleans it."

He was talking about his mom. And his microwave oven.

I half-expected him to pull out a beer bong and invite me to a toga party.

I thanked him for the evening and escaped.

"How was it?" Danielle answered on the first ring as I reached safety in my car moments later.

"Awful. He wanted to know my SAT score."

"What?"

"It was weird. He's in his late thirties, but he sounded like a high school or college kid. His mom cleans his apartment for him. And she lives in Florida! So I'm guessing the floor's a little sticky most of the time.

"Eww." She laughed.

Fast-forward about three months.

"No, Danielle. He's that SAT guy I told you about! Awful. You don't want to go there!"

"Huh?" Danielle was back on Match and looking to fill gaps left after her breakup with Randy.

"That guy I told you about! It's him! The guy who asked me my SAT score. And he said I had bad body language. Remember?"

"Because you were facing away from him?"

"Yeah. I crossed my legs in the opposite direction. So then he starts talking about all the psychology classes he took in college. Danielle, you do *not* want to go out with him!"

"No way!" She laughed.

She spiraled down into his end zone the next night. "It's just a drink. I can't sit here alone tonight!"

I sighed. "1450."

"What?"

"His SAT score."

I heard a laugh. She had me on speakerphone as she

applied makeup.

"Just see if he asks you about your SAT. You might want to look up your old test score. I think that's one of his standard 'get to know you' questions."

"Can't be that bad! Better than sitting home alone!"

She called me on her way home. "Oh my god! He asked me!"

"Your SAT?"

"Yes! I couldn't get out of there fast enough. Honestly, I'm looking forward to being alone in my house with my cat and a movie. That was bad!"

He texted her at 4am. She called me at 7.

"I said 'what the hell?' Can't believe I gave him my phone number."

I couldn't resist. "Tried to warn you…"

The Art of Deletion

I've done it too: Over-communication. I advocate clarity but there's no need for run-on sentences. Punctuate that ending and move on.

It has become a bit of a ritual: The Delete. *"Did you delete him?" "Is he still on your direct dial?" "Did you unfriend him yet?" "Are you ready for **me** to unfriend him yet?"*

While I'm never a proponent of tossing a grenade at the bridge—having formed valued friendships with some of the men who were ultimately not a romantic "click"—there are valid reasons and situations where it will be necessary to pull the pin and hit "delete." However… There is a *huge* difference between the cowardly disappearance we discussed in the last chapter and the choice to do an intentional deletion.

If you've cycled through a breakup and reconciliation scenario three or more times, it's probably time to delete. If he has told you in clear terms that he really isn't interested and you can't quite quit hoping he'll change his mind, hit "delete." If he has shown disrespect toward you or displayed unadmirable qualities you would not tolerate in any other human being, state your intention to cut off communication and then delete him.

Here's why. Transitions are tough. Moving out of a rut takes muscle, determination and focus. Having a tough day at work or a challenge with one of your children—or even a lonely evening at home—can make the last rut you were in look OK again.

But it isn't. You—or he—revved up the motivation to leave it for some valid reasons.

You may forget them. We all do. So leaving yourself opportunities to phone, email, text or cyber-stalk an ex is foolish and self-defeating.

Picture an arid trail. A campground with basic facilities is directly behind you. The path ahead is new terrain. Chances are better than excellent that if you travel far enough, you will discover a better resting place with warm food and hot showers. And it is absolutely true that, with the right attitude, the journey itself will be more enjoyable than backtracking to an empty campsite that lacked full amenities. Life offers more than what is directly behind you, but it will be up to you to find—and recognize—*better*.

While you're on that journey, eliminate temptations to retreat or backtrack. Texting an ex will always sound like a better idea at 11pm than it will at 8:30am. It will seem more reasonable after wine than it will after your morning coffee. If you aren't quite able to delete him yet, do yourself a favor by adhering to a few protective guidelines: 1) Always wait 24 hours before hitting "send," 2) Commit with a friend to talk over temptations before acting upon them, 3) Set up stages of deletion if you can't do the whole thing at once—delete him from your cell phone first, delete social media connections next, and then finally, delete all photos, texts and emails.

Even the tagged Facebook photos I look good in?

Especially the photos you look good in! They will trick your brain into registering an emotional memory as a present tense situation—and the people in that photo grew to be very different, and ultimately, incompatible. Delete.

From the Field: *"Delete Before Disgrace"*

"I texted."

"No! You were doing so well!"

"It was fine. Really. I remembered that I forgot to tell him that a friend of ours got a promotion. And that he left some stuff in my garage..."

"And?" I prompted.

"I just mentioned something about it being great biking weather."

"Danielle!"

"You think that was bad?"

"Well... Have you heard back from him?"

"No," she admitted glumly. "Sent the text three hours ago. Guess I'm not going to hear from him, am I?"

"I doubt it. You kind of broke up, right? I thought you deleted his number and stuff."

"Almost. Thought I had, but it was still on my phone."

"Danielle, you need to delete him completely right now. You don't want to waste another day worrying about whether you're going to hear from him, right? You have better things to do. Delete him. Make a choice to walk away from him."

"You're right. It was kind of a reflex, I guess."

She called me back a moment later, her voice noticeably lighter. "I did it. He's gone."

Building Backbone

Easy breakups are rare and usually indicate a couple has lived in "neutral" for an extended period. In a non-mutual breakup, the weight of sadness is unevenly distributed. The initiator has mentally indexed the reasons for moving on. While the sudden space may be painful and tinged with a little guilt or regret, it's far easier to move toward a new horizon than it is to watch someone walk away. Rarely does the receiver of the "it's not you, it's me" speech think "wrong fit." Instead the resounding message is, "I don't love you anymore," and that hurts.

So you've deleted him. Or are trying to work up the resolve to unfriend him on Facebook and wash the t-shirt he left behind. It's going to take some muscle. You're pushing into a wall of memories and unfulfilled hopes. The impact is painful. But driving on through it, despite the pain of loss, is the only way to disperse its shadow. Here are some strategies for setting yourself back on course.

Revving Out of the Rut

1) Write Out the Reasons. Why it didn't work, what secretly annoyed you, specific instances in which you were unhappy and how you felt about yourself when you were in the relationship. Maybe you were less confident? Resigned? Insecure? Isolated from your friends? Embarrassed by his behavior? Less able to be your true self? Put this all in an email to yourself with the subject line: "Reasons I don't want him anymore."

I kind of hated it when he was so uncomfortable around my friends. He wasn't that great of a kisser... In fact, I didn't really feel as attracted to him when he got swirled by the drama with his ex-wife. I felt guilty for not wanting him more...

He never wanted to listen to my ideas. I am a smart capable woman! He didn't get that. He just seemed to want parts of me—not the whole package...

Be petty. Remember the time he lied to his mom in front of you? Or left you waiting for forty-five minutes at the restaurant without even texting that he'd been delayed? This is the one time and place in your life where *petty* is good, because it will help you focus on your route to better things.

There will be time to forgive and say "Whatever!" later on when you're fully healed.

Send the email to your own address. Flag it and keep resending it—adding new revelations as you gradually discover them buried there under your initial grief. Keep this email visible—to open as needed in those weak moments we all face.

2) Read This Email to a Close Friend. Revealing these inner thoughts makes them real.

Your friend can hold you accountable to them. When you waver, she or he can tell you, "Read the email. He isn't good for you."

Friends usually have a few things to add to your email. I well remember a conversation with a friend after a difficult break-up.

"He drank like a fish every time you left the room!"

"Really? I guess we were pretty unhappy then. I was withdrawing more and more, trying to make it work."

"I could tell *something* was up. He seemed so uncomfortable with himself and everyone else."

"It was a bad time, I guess. I forgot how awful that felt! And he always wanted to drink more than felt good to me! I worried that he might have a drinking problem in those last three months or so."

I got off the phone and typed all of that into my "Reasons I don't want him anymore" email along with some other specific negative memories triggered by our conversation.

3) Get Rid of Reminders. All of them, digital and otherwise. Delete and dump. Did you have a favorite hangout or TV show or special dessert? If it reminds you of him, then set it aside for the time being and replace, reorient and refill with "new." One guy I dated rashly flung his ex-wife's engagement ring into a river. Financially—and legally—it didn't make a lot of sense, but he was focused on moving forward. The ring was a reminder he didn't want or need. Alternately, a friend of mine eBayed a fur coat and other gifts from her ex, and enjoyed spending the cash proceeds. Try to weave logic into your grief and limit the breakage to less valuable items.

4) Get Busy. I don't advocate immediately jumping back into dating, but renew connections that may have suffered while you wallowed through the end of the relationship. Or expand your world a little by doing some of the things you didn't have time for when the ex received so much of your attention. My best remedy has always been to help someone else—residents at my grandmas' nursing homes saw my face more frequently because I had more time available for them. Many of my friends amp up their workouts, take on new responsibilities at work or throw themselves into house projects. Fill your time with good things rather than idle regrets.

Ok… This next one is a little embarrassing, but it works so I'm sharing it.

5) Optional: Create a Breakup Music Mix. No, not the normal tear-inducing sob fest many gravitate toward but rather an empowering and mentally motivating chant-along battle cry. *Hate to stick "cry" in there, but a little crying **will** be part of this exercise.* This will be a workout video for your brain. You're allowed one or two sad songs at the start of the mix—six to ten minutes of pain acknowledgement. Then we add the good stuff. There will be some obvious "good love gone bad" music choices but also include some favorite non-romantic—even danceable—songs into the mix. Look for ones with simple loud choruses into which you can insert your own lyrics with the aim of dismissing the ex. Change a word here and there, and almost any song can be an anthem for change. Curse him, mock him…whatever you need to do to leave him behind. There will be time for forgiveness and kinder more generous feelings later, but the purpose of this music is to rev you out of the rut. Yes, I'm moderately embarrassed to suggest this—acting with kindness is one of my core values—but it's surprisingly effective, and this is about enabling you to make good choices for yourself. So amp up the bass, and make yourself do it once or twice a day. When you're able to sing through three songs in a row, you'll be well on your way to something better. *Now go wash out your mouth with soap!*

6) Buy New Underwear. It needn't be tissue-wrapped expensive. But it should be something exquisitely intimate that makes you feel pretty and that your ex will never ever see. Draw the shades and vacuum in your new lacy thong—*Take that (insert name)!*

And if you still can't move on?

7) Consider Therapy. Many times, that sense of loss may have more to do with other issues from our past—even our childhood. And even if it truly *is* about him? A licensed counselor can help you establish strategies to cope with unwanted change in your life. Making life better again is truly your own choice. [2]

Weathering a Gap Year

Guys get a bad rap for using their nether regions for some of their critical thinking, but women also have an uncanny ability to chase after bad-for-me men for "good sex." *And the definition of "good" can decline dramatically after a few months of sleeping diagonally on your bed.* Complicate this even more with the mixed messages some of us received in our youth along with a marital train wreck or two, and it's no wonder we get confused.

Yes, there are myriad healthful reasons to remain sexually active. It's the ultimate mood enhancer, life extender and can be a great cardio workout. But the benefits to skin, flexibility, blood pressure and inner peace decline dramatically when the sexual activity isn't tied to a quality relationship. Sex for sex's sake is simply an insert A into B move that takes little skill, and offers more risk than reward.

It's *hard* to give up the goodies when you ditch a bad relationship—even though "the goodies" probably weren't that great at the end now, were they?

But back in the beginning when it was amazing...!

Stop right there. The idea is to build healthy forward momentum, not wallow in Photo-shopped endorphins. Yes, endings suck. ALL endings suck—even the ending of a once-good relationship that turned out to be a bad fit for you. Listen: No one likes cleaning out their garage, but you have to get all that crap out of there because you don't need it anymore and you need to make space for a new vehicle. Don't make me send you back to singing that Breakup Music mix again!

My guy friends ask me, "Do you and your girlfriends talk about sex?" and I kind of roll my eyes and give a little shrug. Truly? *Yes, of course we do!* And I think that as adult women, we talk about it *far* more than men. *They* hit the high points in the middle school locker room. Some of *us* didn't find the holy grail until our forties. And one of the big agonies of the newly single woman can include a large portion of sexual frustration.

From the Field: *"I Feel Cheated"*

"You have no idea how different it was back then!" The sweet Irish grandma leaned forward on her bar stool, bending her elbows to clasp the hands of our 40-something bartender. She wasn't talking about automobiles, cell phones or my personal favorite: the microwave oven. Nope, we were talking about sex.

"Then" was the 1940s.

It was a St Paddy's Day drinking night and pints had been poured. "Dan" had asked "Micky" about falling in love with her husband. I had asked her about their first kiss.

"Oh, we didn't do that for a looong time. He held my hand at the movie theater once—I was so scared we'd be seen, I covered our hands with my hat!"

Dan pulled the conversation back to her wedding night, wiping the counter in front of us in order to linger and ignore the rowdy customers at the other end of the bar. Dark haired Dan had poured Micky many drinks over the years, and she seemed to have a little crush on him. I think he reminded her of her late husband.

"I was a virgin."

Dan was incredulous.

"Of course I was! It was the forties! My mother warned me about my wedding night. I was scared to death. I actually clung to the bedpost!"

It was a disturbing visual.

Micky reached for Dan's hand and he gently held hers again. "He, my husband, called his mom to tell her my... um...I guess you'd say my 'reaction.'"

She hung her head. "That's just the way it was, I guess."

I barely knew her, but felt such sorrow. "I'm sorry, Micky. Hope it got better?"

"Not too late," Dan chimed in.

Micky snorted and reached for her beer. "I'm eighty-seven years old. It's over for me. I graduated in '44, got married in '45 and had babies in '46, '47 and '48. I was afraid of sex. No birth control back then. Didn't want to get pregnant again. And he just didn't know any better. Neither of us did."

"Had no idea..." Her eyes were clear but sad. "To tell you the truth, I feel cheated."

Order Backup

A common theme amongst divorced friends is a feeling of having "missed out" during the years spent in a loveless or sexless marriage. *And to those of you newly divorced women who married young and are still silently wondering if good sex is a fairytale—it isn't.* But playing "catch up" in this area exposes you to significant health and emotional risks. Don't let physical needs lead your heart down a dark alley. Patience is not only a virtue—it's grownup wisdom.

A vibrator, safely delivered to your door by Amazon, can help you be patient a little longer. Yep, it's battery-operated and an inferior imitation at that, but it's better than a "wrong guy" for you. *Embarrassing, I know—and I **don't** suggest rating your purchase like you did your book club selections no matter how many stars you see.* A mail order temporary sex toy is discreet and will allow your brain to have more say in the selection process.

Consider it to be your emergency spare tire—good for fifty miles or so, until you can get a proper set of wheels for your vehicle.

Do the Shoulder Shrug

Practice it. A slight lift on one side, a head tip in that direction and a half smile: the Shoulder Shrug. It's the "Well, *that* was different" response you will use for bad dates.

Excruciating small talk will happen, despite your best intentions and screening. The non-click is sadly a more common event than an actual "this could be it", so be ready to frame it in the following positives: 1) It was only an hour—*always keep a first meeting on the short side;* 2) I've knocked one of 7 billion off my list; 3) Wait 'til I tell (fill in the friend).

Truthfully, the best part of many meet-and-greets will be your sense of relief at the closing credits and downloading the dismal details to a friend on the way home.

I thought the date was going rather well until she asked for bail money. She explained that her 15-year old daughter had got caught up with her older boyfriend in a drug scheme. They were both in jail. "Green Eyes" asked if she could "borrow" $10,000 to bail her daughter out. She didn't care what happened to the boyfriend. I did a fantastic job of not spitting a mouthful of coffee on the waiter *and skedaddled. I never figured out if she really had a daughter.*

—my friend Bob

I arrived at the restaurant first and when she came in she was as lovely as her picture, no photo shopping there. We engaged in introductions and pleasantries and began, for me, the arduous task of chitchat. She was polite, articulate, attentive and warm, all good signs right? How would I know? I haven't dated since bell-bottoms! So I did it, I asked if I could see her again… Yeah, silence. Where do I go from here, will I fit under the table? During my short but painful recovery I thanked her for coming to lunch, wished her well and went on my way.

—Brian from Match.com

Adult dating is hard. It will take a few "no thank yous" to get to a "yes please, and thank you very much!" So, keep your heart light and your shoulder limber. Learn something from the experience, and none of it will be wasted time.

From the Field: *"Coffee Carnivore"*

He caught hold of my pinkie finger, gently squeezing it between his forefinger and thumb.

"Worth the drive?"

I smiled. "This is nice." While I usually pad the success ratio of meet-and-greets by setting them for locations proximate to my gym and home grocery store, Sam had talked me into a more secluded Starbucks with a treed patio. And while I classified this second get together as but an extension of our initial abbreviated meeting—I'd been late and he had to leave early—our fingers had been dancing toward one another across the table top. When he went inside to retrieve napkins, I noted his firm physique and thought, "Maybe..."

He leaned across the table to kiss me. There was a spark worth mentioning to my friend Bonnie on the drive home.

"I'd kiss him again."

"That's huge, Heather!"

I shrugged. "Could have been a caffeine buzz. We'll see."

He texted the next morning.

Sam: Wings and beer?

Me: Can't. Have kids. Maybe after the weekend. Wednesday maybe?

And then a couple of days later...

Sam: What were you thinking for tonight?

Me: Oh, Sam. I meant *next* Wednesday. Have a board meeting. Might be able to get together afterward, but I'm not sure how late it will run.

Sam: No worries. Have good meeting and text me after.

Sam: Wish I'd known cause I put on a good shirt... ;)

7:52pm on same day.

Me: Too late?

Sam: No way. Come over. I have wine, nice sunset.

A cold front moved in. Rapidly.

Me: Where?

Sam: Westerville. My home.

Sam: Maybe I should have mentioned. Put load of clothes in. Can't run out now.

Me: Can meet you somewhere in a bit after your clothes are done or we can wait until next week.

Receiving no response I drove home and got ready for bed.

Sam: Real sorry it didn't work out for you.

Me: You understand I hope? Don't know you that well yet.

Sam: Did want to be with you tonight. Well that can't need explanation. Might need context from others you've known...

Me: Coffee was nice. Wanted to get to know you better, but I move slowly. Brain goes first.

Sam: I knew you were a romantic when we kissed. But it doesn't matter. Life is short and I didn't get into you enough to get you to come over.

Sam: Funny. People meet and don't even know...

Sam: How close they were...

Sam: But isn't that life?

Me: Takes time to find things out, Sam, and I have to discover in a way that is comfortable for me too.

Sam: We all have our journeys. So all we can do is see the transactions.

I wondered how hard he was hitting the wine. Or if I was missing some connective texts.

Sam: So there's a dichotomy between what you say and how you act. You can drive down the side of a mountain in a jeep, but you didn't feel safe with me.

My recent adventures in Colorado had been funny over coffee. I struggled to make sense of what felt like an increasingly manipulative man.

Me: This is getting confusing to me. I'm sorry if I offended you, but I have to make choices I'm comfortable with.

Sam: What does coming to my house while I do a load of my kids' laundry have to do with your self-respect?

Sam: Guys use that line on you a lot.

Sam: To my point, I didn't separate myself enough from the guys who must have formed this barrier for you. You're inflexible.

I flinched.

Me: I was willing to meet you anywhere public. Flexible. Your only option was that I come to your house. Inflexible. Still not sure what this was all about, but best of luck to you.

Sam: Couldn't leave house. Simple, not inflexible. Never a question of luck, just focus I suppose…

I looked over the string of texts I had allowed myself to be sucked into for the past hour, realized his laundry was probably dried and folded by then and deleted his number.

Confused. With no glimmer of understanding but some real clarity that Sam wasn't going to work in my life.

I texted Bonnie. "Good kisser is a weird one."

Bonnie: Are you sure??? Sounded promising!

Me: They all do until they open their mouths. Joking!! Kind of…

Zero Waste Dating

At the end of a relationship, good or bad, you should find yourself changed and wiser. Not the *"I'll never date another attorney, that's for sure!"* blanket statements we make to friends when we're angry and avoiding pain, but rather *"I'll be more sympathetic to the scheduling demands of the next guy I date"* or *"Going forward, I won't stick around a guy who doesn't value my time as much as his own."*

I've learned something from every guy I've dated—even those quick grab-a-beer meet-and-greets. Whether information regarding a profession previously unknown to me, an alternate way of thinking about a familiar situation or the deeper stuff of communication and connection, there have been lessons along the way.

Ignoring this information or stuffing it under residual anger or hurt will only delay your progress toward the relationship you hope for. Aim to foster a growing strength and sense of who you really are—but avoid rigidity. It is never "all his fault" when something ends badly. Relationships are a fluid flow. You contributed to the current that took it off course—or maybe you simply chose the wrong no-good-for-you guy again. Figure it out and you'll save yourself a repeat. Similarly, it isn't all *your* fault when a relationship crashes. You have never lost the "perfect man." You're looking for the perfect man for *you*. Remember? A "right fit."

Avoid Pendulum Swings

In an attempt to self-correct a faulty selection process, some of us swing between extremes. Example: After divorcing my straight-laced banker husband, I dated a carefree metal sculpting artist for a while. When that didn't really fit, I sailed back over to a very methodical technical type before swinging on back to yet another "creative."

The better course of action is to fine-tune your essentials. Figure out what it is that drew you to a man and what you actually liked about him while you were in a dating relationship. These may be qualities such as: a sense of fun, curiosity, reliability or compassion. You may have valued a guy's conversational skill or his ability to be comfortably confident in new situations.

Instead of over-correcting for negatives, keep track of these positives. It's information about the kind of man who will click with the woman you are.

Aim For Attainable

From my friend Michael, because—in his own words—*"Seriously, do you know anyone else who has dated over 140 different people during a roughly two year online dating odyssey, LOL?"*

In all of the magic moments over that time period during which I have met these many women, and many of them more than once (even some for a period of months), I have had to come to grips with a sad reality: I have not found that one person who I believe would be 'perfect' for me. And thus, sadly, the realization coalesced that it is not the many candidates out there who do not suit me; it is my failure to have realistic and healthy expectations that is at the root of my failure to connect with 'perfect opportunity.'

* * * * *

"I don't know. It just isn't there for me."
"You said he's funny, attractive and great with his kids. What don't you like about him?"
"He doesn't wear sunscreen."

OK. That last one was me. Maybe I was being a little *too* picky—or in actuality, finding an easy excuse to cut off another *Almost* guy. But ladies, he isn't going to be everything you imagined. Quite simply, your imagination isn't big enough.

After all these years, you know *exactly* what you want, right? Consider that some of the "wants" may stem from what you've become accustomed to and are not necessarily related to what you essentially need.

We are all packages at this point. A guy who loves outdoor activities may not be as ambitious career-wise. Or he might be a career success but less adaptable to situations out of his control. You have to look at the whole guy.

How about you? We tend to think of our own failings as either catastrophes or quirks, depending on whether we've managed to toss off those burdens of guilt and perfectionism. If you view your housekeeping skills as a huge failure, hire some help (or enlist your kids) and accept that you are less attentive to dust than some women. Call it a quirk.

And his desire to nail down details before embarking on a simple trip to the grocery or hardware store? Quirk.

We're all going to have them at this point. The great thing is that some of the quirks will be pretty intriguing and fun. I dated a guy who was into heavy metal—not my taste at all—but who gave his Metallica guitar serenades a classical twist for me. He was also willing to make up and sing dirty lyrics to Karen Carpenter songs with me—fun! Another guy was meticulous in ways I could never be, but never failed to bring backup nutrition bars for me when we hiked or biked—*I accidentally almost fainted in his kitchen once.* Another man had some effeminate qualities I couldn't quite get past but was exceptionally attentive in ways no one else would think to be.

Your model man may come with some features you didn't plan on, but conversely, did you plan on being so picky with your restaurant orders—*Dressing on the side, and could you switch the cheddar for blue cheese and hold the bacon please?*

Most importantly, look for someone who fits you as you are now—or who you are now becoming. Not you as you may have been twenty years ago.

From the Field: *"Here's Who I Was"*

One very muscular arm was draped around a cheetah in his profile photo. Scruffy beard, nice white teeth... I was intrigued. "International security for celebrities and government officials." He'd listed some countries I hadn't even heard of, sounded very active and looked fit.

I created coffee time on my calendar and arranged to meet him at one of the local Paneras I use as a satellite office.

Being a veteran of the coffee meet-and-greet, I situated myself with a view toward the doorway and edited an article on my laptop. I'd be easy to find, and could spot any incoming.

Or so I thought.

I figured the man that limped to my table at the designated time had left something at my booth... But he started removing his jacket and steadied his cane against the booth's side.

"Gary?"

"Hi Heather." We shook hands after he had seated himself.

I couldn't state the obvious. This wasn't the man hugging the cheetah. That man was a scrapbook photo.

"It's been eight years," he revealed as we passed through pleasantries into particulars. "Yeah, I used to have a huge security business. Lots of celebrities, Arnold Schwarzenegger, guys like that. Government officials. My company would provide protection for events and travel, stuff like that. War zones... We did some crazy shit, but it was very lucrative. Until the accident..."

"What happened?"

"Well, I was taking a shower in a New York hotel and the light blew out. I was electrocuted. I'm lucky to be alive, but it burned my insides, injured my spine, internal organs… There's nerve damage." He winced. "I'm always hoping medical science will come up with something new, but I basically had to sell my business and retire on the lawsuit settlement."

I tried not to let my jaw drop further than polite, but I was horrified. "I'm so sorry! How difficult for you!"

He shrugged. "Life's a little different now. I have all these great cars but have to use a driver. Can't drive them myself anymore. And well… Everything still works, if you're wondering about that at all."

I hadn't been, but nodded. Embarrassed, but striving to show at least mild appreciation.

It was our only meeting, but it twisted my emotions. If I'd known him before his accident, been his girlfriend perhaps… I'd have been helping him move onward through this challenge. But to be presented with his medical trials now, in this deceptive manner, made it hard to imagine coming alongside his journey forward. Presenting *Reality* might have cut down his chances for making dates with women online, but I wondered how many times he could bear explaining the discrepancy face-to-face.

His online profile was an eight-year old time capsule. Historical.

Funny, but my mind leapt to another Match guy I'd corresponded with: Mitch. Mitch freely shared that a diving accident had left him without the use of his legs, but he wrote that he was still a great dancer and would even give the right lady a ride home on his chair. He reached out to me, and we corresponded a couple of times even though he lived almost an hour away. He was funny, genuine and comfortable in his own skin.

And given a choice, I knew I'd have enjoyed walking alongside Mitch in his chair over riding with Gary in the backseat of his luxurious cars reminiscing about a past I never knew.

Recognize Relationship Models

Amy sighed and spooned her soup. "I don't know. I guess I want what my parents have."

"Good marriage?"

"Kind of perfect actually."

My own experience was more opposite hers, and yet we were each guided—for better or worse—by what we watched as children.

Don't underestimate the power of those early observations. Whether you witnessed positive or negative behaviors—or a mix of both—they were performed by your chief authority figures, and chances are good that those registered responses were still in your toolbox when you got married. "Normal" will be whatever you are accustomed to, whether within the ballpark of acceptable and respectable or not.

Whether your parents' marriage was "perfect" or neighbored hell, identify it as *their* marriage. Your next long-term relationship should follow the model *you* craft with the man *you* choose to build it with. The same goes for comparisons to the marriages of your friends, family and those lived out in the tabloids or on reality TV. Being aware of your expectations will allow you to dial them down to "reasonable."

Amy's dad brought her mom breakfast in bed, held her

hand and fixed things in the house before she even knew them to be broken. In Amy's words, "he basically worshipped her." It would be reasonable for Amy to look for an affectionate man over a man who saves his kisses for the bedroom, and seeking an atmosphere of mutual admiration and respect is essential. But it's a bit unreasonable for her to wait on an adoring mind reader. And the truth is, that what she saw of her parents' marriage is what they permitted her to see—in all likelihood, her parents experienced the same moments of boredom and disappointment that all of us occasionally experience over the long haul. What's important to note is that they were (and are) committed to something bigger than their individual selves and that they maintain civil behavior toward one another no matter how or where they may disagree.

My own parents had a very challenged relationship. That they ultimately remained married is a testament to discipline and, again, a devotion to something larger than their individual desires. But where Amy's parents' marriage served to set her bar excessively high, observing my parents' patterns set my own expectations for loving communication unreasonably low. Towards the end, as my father was dying, their devotion to one another grew more obvious. But that new information came thirteen years into my marriage—already modeled after the non-communicative, "no waves; no worries" veneered facsimile I'd grown up on. My marital failure rests solidly upon the mistakes of my ex-husband and myself, but it is interesting to see how we aimed low, achieved "low" and ultimately could not live with the results. Pre-marital counseling, while helpful, only uncovered the thought patterns we were able to access within ourselves, and at that point in our young lives, we had closed off the information we most needed to find.

Taking a few minutes to review and discuss your

expectations with a friend may help you avoid missing a good thing or chasing after someone you really won't want in the end.

CHAPTER NINE

Is This Thing Working?

SETTLING INTO A RHYTHM where habits are learned—and created together—can feel pretty good, especially after a dry or, conversely, "anecdotally rich" dating period. It may just feel "right." Or it may feel "right" compared to where you've been. You owe it to yourself (and him) to figure that out before you've invested months of time into the new relationship.

From The Field: *"I Don't Know If We're a Couple"*

"Of *course* you are! You've been seeing Bill, and only Bill, for over a year. You're sleeping together. It's the best sex you've ever had. You—"

"He hasn't said 'I love you.' That's important to me, and if he can't say it, how can I be sure we're really a couple?"

"Bonnie…He's an IT guy! You knew that going in! You said that just isn't his personality!"

"But, I need to know if we're a couple!"

We'd had this conversation many times.

My logical suggestion to positively reinforce the occasional attentive behavior she craved—"*That makes me feel so special when you grab my arm. Makes me wanna grab your…*"—made sense to her. But verifying with Bill that he wasn't seeing anyone else sent Bonnie into turmoil.

"He broke up with me, remember?"

"That was a year ago, right?"

"Yeah, but we'd just had THE MOST romantic weekend, I started to relax and said, 'It kind of feels like we're a couple,' and he panicked! He BROKE UP WITH ME!"

We were walking a normally less traveled trail, but unfortunately startled a couple of bird watchers with that proclamation.

"He said he needed to see other people! He got on Match! He—"

"Bonnie, he panicked. You said so yourself. This was a year ago. Just in the time I've known you, he's stepped up his game. He plans for you. You talk every day. He's excited about taking you on the fishing trip and introducing you to something he loves. He obviously made a choice that you are the woman he wants to spend his time with!"

"Unless he's still on Match."

"You think he is?"

"No. But he COULD BE! He hasn't said he ISN'T!"

"Bonnie, you have to either trust that he loves you by the way he treats you or push your relationship questions into an actual conversation. You're rolling around in this!"

"I'm scared."

"I know."

I patted her shoulder.

"He broke up with me."

"I know. But you guys are at a different place now."

"I think I have trouble trusting after the divorce."

Three months later...

"It's good to know he sees us as a couple, but I just don't know..."

"Because...?"

"The sex is sooo good. What if *that's* the reason I'm staying with him?"

"Do you think it is?"

We were walking laps at my gym this time. I glanced at the guy just behind us, hoping he was cranking his music loud enough to miss whatever was coming next. He was ogling a blonde trotting a treadmill.

"Well... I mean I've never had such an easy time in bed with ANYone. It's just so natural, and he really excites me."

"That's good!"

"But we don't talk like you and John do."

"John and I are different people. We probably like to talk a lot more than the average couple."

"That's probably true. There are times we don't say anything at all, and that's OK. It's comfortable... But what if it's just because I'm addicted to the sex?"

Two months later.

"Jim is texting again."

Jim was the first guy Bonnie had dated after her wrenching divorce.

"He knows you're seeing Bill, right?"

"Yeah. It's light stuff. Probably shouldn't though, right?"

"Would it bother Bill?"

"Probably."

Bonnie was quiet for a minute and then asked about a mutual friend who seemed to be inducing a crash/burn on her relationship.

"I'm not sure she knows what she wants yet," I commented. "It can take some time to figure that out, and he's the first guy she's dated."

"Like Bill."

"Except for Jim."

"Well, yeah." We turned a corner and jokingly planned an intervention on a woman sporting a well-sprayed 80's hairstyle.

"So..."

I'd known there was something. Bonnie is pretty transparent.

"Bill kind of surprised me the other night. Sexually."

"Good surprise or weird stuff?"

"Well, weird to me, I guess."

She described it to me, and I winced.

"I just kind of bit the pillow, and then we kind of moved on. But I read about it online. Not comfortable with it *at all*. What do I do if he wants to try that again? I'm afraid he's getting bored. My friend Debi's boyfriend got all weird on her after they got married and—"

"First of all. If you don't want to do something, you say so, Bonnie. 'I'm just not comfortable with that. Let's find something that works for both of us.'"

"Don't know if I could do that."

"It's *your body*, Bonnie. Of course, you can do that!" I love Bonnie but sometimes wish I could just backfill the gaps in her self-confidence. "Look, you can either bring it up and explain it wasn't comfortable for you, or you can just wait and see if it comes up again and be prepared to say, 'no thanks.'"

"I don't know if he was just curious or is getting bored."

"From what you've told me about your sex life, it doesn't sound like boredom is an issue. I think it's good that the two of you can be kind of open to trying things, but you just need to be equally open about your comfort level."

She was quiet.

"I don't know..."

"You're excited about the Florida trip, right?"

"Yeah, that will be fun."

"He's trying to make that special for you."

"Yeah..."

"Well. At some point, you'll have to decide this is the guy you want to work with or that this guy is too much work. Either jump all the way in, or get out and give each of you the chance to find a better fit."

"January..."

We'd talked about that before too. Between work, her ex-husband and kids, her life was too crazy for major decision-making at the moment.

"Sounds like a plan."

Developing or Diminishing?

Two basic questions that help in gauging relationship quality might be: "How do you feel when you're with him?" and "How do you feel when you're away from him?" Good relationships tend to reveal and develop our possibilities. Unhealthy ones spotlight our flaws and shortcomings.

Ted was a classic Cling Wrap guy, and the longer we were

together, the less confident and secure he grew. He is a good guy, so I blamed myself. In an effort to help us "fit," I tried nudging him into revealing more of his true feelings but he seemed afraid to show anything other than what he thought I wanted to see. We had invested some time in the relationship—it seemed essential to do everything possible to make it work. I tried diminishing myself to allow him more opportunities to lead, but instead of running with them, he shrunk with me. I respected him less and less—and as I became less than the fairly strong woman he had been attracted to initially, his fascination waned as well. We spiraled down together, both becoming less than our original single selves.

After leaping into back row seats on the wrong metro train in Paris—my idea, no doubt—and smelling more sickly sweet pot than sweaty body odor, we noticed some younger tough-looking Parisians congregating in the SRO section by the car exits. These were no accidental meetings. The young men passed around lit joints and made other more furtive exchanges. Ted and I quickly realized our mistake and the need to switch lines in four stops to reverse our current direction away from the city.

We also became aware that while we had blended fairly well within Paris proper, here on a train headed toward the projects and less prosperous suburbs, we stood out as Americans—prime targets for pickpockets and worse.

Four stops…

I threw back my shoulders and kept my cross-body purse tucked discreetly behind my back against the seat. After pointedly making eye contact with a couple of the guys crowding the exit, I glanced reassuringly over at Ted seated to the left and across from me. *We'll be fine. We can do this.*

Rigid-backed, staring straight ahead, he didn't even see me. *Damn. I have to save **both** of us!!*

No, there was no dramatic ending beyond my recognition of that pivotal moment a couple of months later. Our exit came; we made it onto the right metro train and trekked back to our hotel.

But I mulled over that event—wondering why I couldn't let go of it and what it really meant. A few months earlier, Ted's protector instinct might still have kicked in, but upon reflection, it became clear to me that our relationship was making him less of the man he wanted to be. He eventually reached the same conclusion and disappeared at the start of the New Year.

From the Field: *"Amy's Italian"*

"So you like him?" I aimed for a neutral tone. Amy had just described a self-absorbed and unappreciative man. But he had hooked her with great sex, an Italian accent and a few random promises.

"Yeah. He's..." I waited, cell phone to my ear, as Amy twirled through the descriptive words that would counterweight his inattentiveness to her own needs and feelings. She settled on, "He makes me happy."

"How so?"

"Well, when we're together he is sooo thoughtful, and honestly, the sex is *amazing!*"

I waited.

"We had a great time last weekend—did dinner, the galleries and a movie—but, it's Wednesday, and I've heard nothing from him! Well, there was a text yesterday... 'Hope you're having a great week' or something like that."

"I really like him," she continued.

"But?"

"But I feel bad! It's like he ignores me when we aren't together. And I always have to make the plans for us. He doesn't initiate *anything* unless it's last minute, and then he just comes over and we end up in the bedroom. Or the kitchen. Or the family room..." she laughed. "He gets together with his friends every Sunday. He doesn't invite me," she said sadly.

"What do you like about him?"

"Well, he's really sweet when we're together. I'm afraid I'm not good enough for him though. Even though I *know* I'm better than anyone else he'll ever meet!"

"Amy! You're amazing. You're smart, beautiful, funny, successful... Why would you ever not be good enough for him?!"

"Sometimes he squeezes my love handles. He wants me to do a boot camp with him. It's always a joke, but I think *he* thinks I'm overweight. Maybe that's why he doesn't want me to meet his friends..."

"And then he doesn't call..."

"No." Amy sighed.

"He makes you feel like less than who you are, Amy." She sighed again.

Building Trust

Ramping up again is hard. Don't you wish there were an upload option? Or that we could store all the good stuff from the last relationship to "the Cloud" for ready access as needed instead of starting from scratch again?

Some withhold critical information—like my breakfast

date who sheepishly revealed that his divorce was only a week old. Others spill too quickly, revealing all their sins or hopes of love to see how quickly you'll leave.

Pacing the pour takes poise. It takes trust to build trust. You have to have some faith in your own instincts as well as in your ability to handle potential disappointment to even begin the process. For many of us, it's a balky start. Our eagerness for intimate connection slams against residual memories and fears from every unhappy ending we've ever known.

Separating the "good information" from the pain of past romantic experiences will allow us to act thoughtfully rather than react instinctively.

Trust is not a flip decision. It's rather the dimmer switch that brightens the room as you make discoveries that confirm your hopes. Simply flipping on "trust" for a stranger is foolish—and a little disrespectful of yourself. There's no need to fold your arms across your chest and wait for his first misstep. That's a bit paranoid and unattractive. Instead, view the journey into dating as a series of revelations that will either draw you forward on a path or allow you to change direction as needed.

Maintaining Your Own Life

Don't be the disappearing friend. You (*used to*) know her, remember? She was in your life 24/7 until she met a man, and then she vanished, assumedly to be in *his* life 24/7. But never fear, she'll return if the new relationship takes a dive… Only to disappear one more time if it achieves buoyancy again.

Ladies, value your female friendships. And if the ones you have aren't worthwhile and uplifting, expand your circle. Your life must remain bigger than your plans for Saturday night or your happiness will be determined by something over which you have little control. Don't give up book club and yoga and all those other pieces of your life that have made you the woman you are after you attract your new guy. When you meet a man you want to spend time with, aim for gradual adjustments rather than a total reroute of your life. Dropping friends and regular activities to mold your life into his schedule demonstrates a lack of self-esteem. It's a needy whining statement of: "I'm not genuine. I've been going through the motions trying to meet you, and now that you're here, I don't have to fake this anymore."

When you meet *that guy*, there should be a *blending*, not an *ending* of all that came before. If you are genuinely enjoying a good life, he will enhance it, not eclipse it. Value yourself by maintaining some separate activities. This demonstrates self respect, will give you a little time to miss one another (which is a good thing) and facilitate a valuable inflow of new ideas. Couples that completely cocoon from the world eventually run out of things to talk about and get bored with one another—and have to start the dating process all over again!

Growing Together

In a mutually fulfilling and healthy relationship, the two of you will truly add up to something more than either of you alone. Because you will both be bringing something of value: your experiences, positive attitudes, willingness to learn and passion to grow. You will facilitate opportunities for each of you to become a better person. And that combination of the two of you will be capable of bigger things than either of you on your own.

Alternately, if one or both individuals have viewed couplehood as the "achievement," rather than a means of further enhancing and growing their lives, the relationship will shrivel in upon itself like a slowly deflating balloon.

What we bring into a relationship is finite and will eventually be fully consumed unless we continue to pursue our passions, individually and jointly. What doesn't grow will begin to whither and eventually die, which is the sad story of many first marriages.

You have the chance to build something better next time. This time. Be wary of repeating old mistakes.

"His friends" and "her friends" will ultimately become "your friends," and you will hopefully find new friends together. Romantic evenings by the fire are lovely unless they become routine at which point they will no longer be romantic at all. Go out in the world together. Give yourselves new things to discover and talk about.

Family Blending

At some point—long after that first kiss and whispered "I love you"—when you begin planning a future together, it will be time to begin the most important life blending of all: your children.

Anecdotally, more relationships seem to falter on children than on financial issues. Parenting styles, exes and personalities are all factors that can drive a loving relationship into the battle zone.

Begin slowly by meeting the other's children—without your own kids—and vice versa. Don't do this until you know this man's history and have had to talk through some differences of opinion. Your kids don't get the *Almost* guys.

Beginning to spend time with one another's children will be another step in your decision process. That strong guy you've grown to love may be a weaker parent than you'd like. Or he may be stricter than you are—or completely inconsistent. If you don't respect his parenting, it will impact your relationship. Somehow, the two of you will need to navigate these differences. Or walk away and wait for someone with whom that will be possible.

If and when your kids are separately comfortable with each adult, you can begin thinking about joint activities. The ages of your children and the tenor of the divorce will make a huge difference in this whole process. Younger children and older children may be less concerned about mommy or daddy dating than those in late elementary and middle school, but that isn't always the case.

Keep the first meeting short and loosely structured: Bowling or a trip to the zoo are easy choices depending on the ages of your children. Once you start this process, try to schedule regular get-togethers to foster relationship building. *Remember that if you each have two kids, the two of you are actually nurturing nine new relationships!* It may be worth investing in some counseling sessions to strategize and unify before you begin or during the process. Expect to labor a little. Love takes even more work the second time around.

Some basic ideas to consider: 1) Mom and Dad are the parents. Do not parent one another's children beyond basic "house rules" you have previously discussed. 2) Be as fair and even-handed as you can possibly be. Yes, your kids (and possibly your partner) will keep score. Try not to keep score yourself. 3) Be parents first, but make sure to retain "couple" time. Keep it sacred, because everything rests upon your relationship. Should you decide to marry, your goal should be to model a better sort of loving relationship than your kids witnessed in your first marriages.

Dishonest View of Self

No one can know you until *you* know you. Until you are comfortable with who you are you're introducing a stranger. Think to those awkward moments when you're fumbling for a name—same sort of thing. So you need to get past who your ex-husband thought you were, who your parents and siblings think you are—and get real with yourself.

Few of us think too highly of ourselves. Life has a tendency to knock the over-esteemed down to level ground where they can mingle with the rest of us. The problem is that, usually, we view our self-portraits with a magnifying glass superimposed over our flaws. We see the deficits rather than the accentuating features.

But the truth is we all have some pretty cool accentuating features! They may not be the ones you would have chosen, but you might have chosen the very ones you *have* if they hadn't been yours to begin with—we're funny that way.

For some of my friends, it's second nature to throw a dinner party in less than twenty-four hours. Me—I'd need a couple of weeks, a lot of help, dim lighting and guests that had enjoyed a "really big lunch" before they came over. My daughter used to grab the parent sign-up forms in elementary school, draw a line through crafts and snacks and write me in for games. That's me. I'm OK with that. I can throw things together and feed people, but I look more elegant in hiking sandals than oven mitts.

But I also know what I'm good at, and that makes me confident. Knowing your strengths allows you to angle the lighting a little. *No one* has the whole package—not possible. *And we probably wouldn't like them if they did, so they'd have no girlfriends, which would isolate them in a showcase all by themselves.*

So celebrate yourself a little. Write down your "positives":

Anything from "great skin" to "I can change a bike tire." This is YOU! You have a lot to offer the right guy—and the whole world—once you define and embrace those strengths. They won't match anybody else's package. Think: *I am a snowflake!*

Integrity Gap

There are few dating situations more disheartening than an "I'll call you" that never happens. I remember well the words of my artist friend who was similarly frustrated with me, "If someone wants to see someone, they find a way, Heather." He was hurt, and he was right. While I sometimes described myself as being on a "slow boil" (as long as the water was getting warmer, I lingered), the fact is that I spent a lot of time simply dating the wrong guys. My heart was never fully engaged, so my caring words didn't match my growing desire to gain space from my "beloved."

So…if he says he'd like to get together but never actually arranges it and gets off the phone quickly when you mention it? Shrug your shoulders, chalk it up to bad timing or his emotional glitch and walk away. His response does not define or change who you are. He may simply be the wrong fit for your life. Delete his number and text messages so that you won't be tempted to chase after the red herring. There will be someone better. There always is. We'll look at ways to expand your network and grow your dating opportunities in the next chapter.

Light Lifting or Heavy Labor?

Building and maintaining a relationship is hard, but while

working through details may cause you to break a sweat occasionally, the cardio should—mostly—be confined to the bedroom.

We make it a lot harder than it needs to be. A bad relational fit will be as difficult as sliding the proverbial square peg into a round hole. There will be no melding without a lot of abrasion, and it will always be a little "off" because it wasn't right to begin with.

Walk away from these situations. We have a hard time standing with empty hands, but how will you ever be available for the right things in your life—men and otherwise—if you're distracted, working to make a subpar situation livable? Those hands need to be actively working to build the life you want to live in.

If the arguments or doubts have a connective theme: he ignores you, you don't completely respect him, you wonder if he has a drinking problem… These are reinforcing data worthy of consideration.

I broke up with one guy three times for the same basic reason. My eventual withdrawal—in response to the situation—eventually made him flee. Best for both of us, but I could have saved us both a lot of heartache by listening to my intuition—and my friends.

On the other hand, if you're emotionally connected and just dealing with the occasional misunderstanding or scheduling glitch? Pass this book on to a girlfriend who needs it!

CHAPTER TEN

~⌒~

CREATING CONNECTION IN YOUR LIFE

FROM TIME TO TIME, as we collectively indulge in 20/20 hindsight, I've laughingly suggested to women that it might be effective to run some of our relational decisions by a "tribunal" of friends—because what can be glaringly obvious when written out in a book like this can be surprisingly difficult to navigate individually. And while one friend's gentle suggestion will move sand as a single wave, groups of friends might be able to help themselves, individually, to change the tide.

At the least, we need to give serious time and effort to rebuilding our post-divorce lives before we get swept into premature dating decisions.

From the Field: "*Should I Go Tackle Him?*"

Bonnie is one of my regular walking buddies. We laugh a lot, try not to pee our pants when we get on a good roll and scheme about how we'll win "The Amazing Race" someday. I'm limited to three-mile trail runs following my last ankle surgery, but we've worked out how to walk most of the trails together and still include my running time on one of the loops.

I'd just finished my three and found her on a back trail where we resumed our conversation.

"I just don't see it happening. I've met a lot of guys. I get *approached* by a lot of guys, but it's been almost two years now. I'd just like to want to *kiss* someone! That never happens. I need a smart guy who can make me laugh. Make me think. With more of a world-view. In good shape. Who's interested in other people and places and art and music and—"

"Younger," Bonnie pitched in. "Because you've got so much energy and look ten years younger. Bitch." She smiled.

"See what I mean? It's too much! He *doesn't* live in Columbus. I'm not even sure he lives in *America!*"

"Heather, you're beautiful, you're smart, you're in great shape..." Bonnie is a great affirmer.

"Not helping me, Bonnie. It's OK. I mean—my life is better now than it's ever been. Even when I'm *not* dating anyone. *Ever!* But honestly, I just don't even feel like trying sometimes. It's more fun to go out dancing with you and Adrianne or to hit happy hour with all the girls than waste time on another bad date."

"Just takes one."

"Now *there's* a new cliché!" I smiled at her. "Seriously, I just think it gets harder the more you like yourself! I really don't want to settle now. Yeah, it's been 'two years,' but I've also *waited* 'two years.' Why stop now? I miss being touched and, you know, being planned for... I do *everything*. Kids, school/sports, house, work, finances... And I suck at most of it because it's just too much for one person." I winced. "Eww. I'm whining—"

"No, you're not. Just venting."

"Well, sounds like whining to me. Hurt *my* ears! Think I'm just exhausted. Just about all of the time. Like we *all* are. Good thing we have our friends!"

"I think you need to let *me* pick him out for you."

"Oh Bonnie, you'd pick out some thirty-year old because he looks like a good dancer or some eighty-year old with a Viagra prescription just to be mean!"

"I would not!"

"I know. We probably *could* pick better for each other than we do for ourselves."

Bonnie tipped her head toward me. "How about him?"

"Huh?"

"The guy—" She shut up and smiled awkwardly as a roughly handsome, dark-haired man walked by, and then whispered furiously. "Him! What did you think? He's your type, isn't he?"

I nodded.

"Too short?"

I shook my head.

"Want me to go tackle him for you?!"

I nodded.

Bonnie looked back. "Aww...he's too far now. I'd have to run."

Cabernet Coaches

In the first few months after my divorce my calendar had huge overwhelming blocks filled with kids' activities abutting vast empty spaces in which to mope, work and then mope some more. I could usually kick the moping with running and biking, but solitary dinners felt lonely and my dog Lily was a poor conversationalist.

My next stage was a venture into online dating. Emails flew, my phone buzzed constantly and I filled my calendar. Gradually, I began finding similarly single girlfriends, but it was hard. I didn't really know how to make friends as a 40-something woman. Married friends and acquaintances were busy with their families. I was pretty certain I was the only divorced woman in central Ohio.

Little did I know that we were all hiding helplessly in our homes, hoping someone would find us.

Building a network of single (and married) women friends is critical to creating a good life. It will take many—some will come and go—so never stop reaching out. It isn't pathetic to look for new friends—it's grownup behavior that will make your life better in almost every way.

I used to dread filling out medical forms because of that big space for emergency contacts. I had none. My ex? Don't think so. The friends and family who were furious with me for divorcing my ex? No again. I usually scribbled in a contact with a wrong phone number, because I didn't want an emergency room nurse to hear "Heather who?" if I had an unfortunate accident. I had no ICE (In Case of Emergency) contact number on my phone.

Recently, however, I went through major surgery that resulted in eight weeks of crutch use and no driving, and it was a breeze. My friends dropped in daily and hauled me everywhere I needed or wanted to go: to the grocery, the gym, dress shopping, to happy hours… Frankly, it was much easier than my previous surgery ten years ago when I'd relied on two friends and my then husband.

The difference? In the past couple of years, friends—especially the ones I like to think of as my Cabernet Coaches—became my relational priority right after my children. Dating is a bit further down the list—but as I grow my life, I expand my possibilities.

From the Field: *"Disbanded Romeo"*

Dawn perused the crowd with a critical eye. "I see a few possibilities here." She nodded toward a cluster of golf-attired men in a corner of the bar, relaxed in an advanced state of beer hydration.

"You think?"

"Yes, I think," she grinned at me. Dawn was on a mission to move me from my sequestered sideline seat back into dating. An especially busy season of work and kids' sports activities had sapped my meet-and-greet motivation. My online profile had been hidden for weeks, and she had decided it was time to kick my butt back off the bench, in the same manner that I frequently attempted to yank my friend Danielle to the sidelines for a breather.

Married herself, Dawn was fully focused and selective in a way many of my single women friends can't be—acting more as my personal shopper than a general crowd browser.

We settled onto stools with burgers and drinks and did some people watching as we caught up on the past week. Men began wandering up or simply pausing as they worked their way through the crowded room. We eliminated the ones that wobbled, and after a full day of golf tournament parties, there were many of those.

Watching a younger guy attempt to draw women via his resemblance to Tom Cruise was mildly amusing, but wearing dark glasses in the dimly lit bar made it difficult for him to properly identify his targets.

Finally an attractive forty-something ambled over and made a stab at small talk. I swiveled around to chat while Dawn continued eating, ears on alert.

He opened with a compliment, "I love your hair!"

My hair isn't that remarkable—wavy, auburn and generally a bit wind-blown as I prefer fresh air to air conditioning, but I thanked him.

"So were you at the tournament today?" he asked referring to the Memorial Tournament at Muirfield Village Golf Club.

"Nah, I had to work."

"Me too. Client outing," he smiled.

"Nice remote office space," I commented.

We mined the basics, hitting hometowns, our present suburban locations and college alma maters.

"Kids?" I asked.

"Three girls."

"Boy, girl, boy for me."

We bantered a bit. The bar swelled with inebriated newcomers and the noise level went up. He leaned his ear to my mouth to hear a response, resting a hand lightly on my shoulder.

Dawn swung around. "So," she glanced down at his ringless left hand. "You're single?" She glanced at me, "You covered that?"

I nodded awkwardly. "He has three daughters. Mike, this is Dawn."

They shook hands. Mike offered to buy us beers.

"I'm just drinking water tonight. So, you're divorced Mike?"

I cringed at Dawn's over-protectiveness. I had already done the standard delving to determine marital status. This was overkill.

"Well," he shifted uncomfortably and gave me an awkward glance. "No."

I sat up and looked away.

"Where's your wedding ring, Mike?" Dawn could be relentless.

His left hand was now stuffed into his khaki shorts pocket. Digging.

"What?" He pulled his hand out, a gold band loosely slipped onto his ring finger. "I'll go grab those beers," he mumbled.

"Yeah. You do that," Dawn smiled sweetly.

We swung to face one another as he slipped away into the crowd.

"Dawn! He acted like he was single!"

"He wasn't wearing a ring when he walked up. I checked." Dawn gave me a grim smile.

"I can't believe that just happened. I gave him every opportunity to say he was married. He nodded like he was divorced as well when I answered that I'd been single for five years."

"Think he'll bring you back that beer?"

I laughed drily. "He'd be an idiot to come back and face you again!"

"How many kids?"

"Three daughters. Probably listening to bedtime stories with mommy while he's prowling this bar." I shuddered. Not in judgment of *his* behavior so much as at the fact that I'd unintentionally enabled a breach in his marital relationship for even that brief moment. "Poor wife…"

Dawn patted my hand. "Not your fault."

"I'd never go there again."

"I know," she said.

I ordered my own beer.

Stability and Perspective

Look at you juggling your kids' basketball practices and guitar lessons, managing your finances and work and home maintenance, fitting in workouts and grocery runs and doctor visits… It's grueling. No one but another single woman will truly understand how hard your life can be at times.

But it can be very very good. There's that sense of accomplishment when you finish a big work project, land a new client or get promoted. And that swell of parental pride when your child grows closer to his or her potential. And that moment when you fall into bed and think, "I'm exhausted, but I did it! Not all of it, but what I absolutely had to do today? Done!"

Without a broad support base, however, it's easy to get stuck in the stress mode where nothing you do will ever be enough.

Our friends help us through the wobbles: *"So, you'll pick up store bought cookies for school this time. Crumb up the edges, and no one will know."* They provide life-saving perspective: *"You're doing the best you can. This is a really hard time, but I have faith in you. Let's get together next weekend?"*

To expect yourself to maintain a positive attitude and

momentum all by yourself is unreasonable. *You're good, but you're not **that** good…*

Preventing "Stupid"

Our friends can nudge us in better directions when we "know better." But we have to give them permission to speak. Affirming friends are good, but friends who aren't afraid to tell you what you need to hear are even better. A couple of "What are you thinking?!" friends are essential to building your best possible life. They will help hold you accountable to stated goals and principals. My very best friends have pledged to tell me when I should stop wearing a bikini. I work out a lot, but that "Heather, why don't you try on a one-piece" day will come, and I don't want to miss it by a minute!

Singles without "What are you thinking?!" friends are the ones who are met with averted eyes at the gym because of their inappropriate clothing. Their gray roots glimmer and their hot pink thongs are exposed through the back of their foldable chairs on the sideline at your kids' soccer games. They date married men waiting for "someday" and pay too much for their oil changes. They need *you* to become their friend or steer them to other women with whom they might connect.

From the Field: *"The Percocet Proposal"*

She blamed the marriage on a bike wreck and painkillers, but Danielle's relationship with Randy had boomeranged between heaven and hell with whiplashing frequency during the entire three years since we first met at the gym.

While their initial endings included wistful longings and teary promises, the last few severing attempts were shoulders-down-aim-for-the-finish-line endeavors.

"I left a note on the garage door. He'll see it. Don't you think he'll see it?"

"You don't want to talk to him?"

"No. Too rough. This is the only way."

And she was right. Texts led to phone calls, which led to final meetings, which led to resigned "new beginnings."

"I know him. It's what I've chosen," she'd sigh.

"You love him?"

"I guess so. Can't imagine life with anyone else."

But what if that's just a simple lack of imagination?

The breakups became almost cyclical toward the end. I'd set a mental clock with each reunion and wait. Within a couple of weeks they would hit their stride and then "the drift" would commence anew.

"We're good," Danielle would say and then move on quickly to talk about work and her kids.

A week or two later, I'd note the gradual deflation as she began buckling under his need to instill his sense of order in her house. "You know Randy!" she'd grimace. "He isn't comfortable with large groups." Or, "He freaked out when I was frying the chicken. He stood behind me with a roll of paper towels to blot up the grease." She laughed—but while it was funny, it didn't sound fun. There were issues with their kids, with her money. Randy had a better idea for every one of Danielle's.

Finally, they broke it off for real. Danielle kept her blinders on, ignored his texts and sprinted into a new relationship. I wasn't wild about her new "distraction" as she called him, but she seemed much healthier minus the added weight of Randy's demands. She even started frying chicken again.

Then came the bike wreck.

She called me from the hospital, and I raced to the ER. Her collarbone was broken, and the whole experience had shaken her up. Her bike spokes had tangled with tape floating from a recently paved driveway and her routine bike ride on the quiet country roads near her home had suddenly left her, a single mom, very aware of her own vulnerability.

The worst was yet to come in her master bath three days after the wreck. Danielle looked in the mirror and noticed a lack of symmetry. The bike accident had not only flattened her confidence, it had also deflated one of her breast implants.

She called me. "I think it's leaking." Her voice was soft. Expressionless.

"Are you sure?"

"Yeah. My left side is draining. I have to get it replaced." Her voice rose, "I haven't even paid for the hospital visit, and now I have to replace an implant! Those are expensive! And I'll be laid up for a while. How am I supposed to do this?"

"I'll help you. You know I'll help you, Danielle. And there's Megan and Marie and..." I began listing her friends.

"Do I tell him?"

"Randy? Of course not!"

"No. Sam."

I suspected he wouldn't last and hadn't committed his name to brain space yet.

"And what do I say at work?!"

I heard her crumbling inside and tried to stay close the next few days. After her surgery the nurse gave us aftercare instructions and a bottle of Percocet. I drove Danielle home, her daughter arrived to keep an eye on her that first night and Danielle began her recovery.

It hurt. And it was hard. She hit the Percocet during the week and invited me over for wine that Friday night.

"Are you allowed to drink with the medication?"

"I'm only having one glass and it's not like I'm going to drive anywhere!"

I went over to keep her company.

Within ten minutes, she broke the news.

"I called him."

"Sam?"

"No. Randy. I had a weak moment and texted. He texted back. He was worried about me. I called. And he came over for a while last night."

Internally, I sighed.

"He's different. *We're* different. And I can't do this alone, Heather."

"But you *aren't* alone," I pointed out. "You have at least three friends who will drop anything to come and help you!"

"I need *him* right now."

I dropped it.

They were engaged two months later and married six months after that. And within seven months of saying "I do," Danielle said, "I don't." She virtually disappeared during the brief marriage, trying her hardest to make the best of her mistake. The divorce finalized within the same calendar year.

She blames the Percocet.

Regifting: He Might Be Good for Her

When we're able to make dating choices "yes/no" decisions, we become less territorial and can effectively widen that two-lane relationship road into a mega-highway of connective possibilities.

This is a primary reason to avoid bridge burning—*Well, that and the fact that you'll like your own self better if you guardrail your words with kindness.*

Mike and Mary? Maybe. George and Kara? I've thought about it. One of my neighbors and Danielle? Maybe not… The charming chemist, the good-hearted artist, the straight-up high school psychologist who loves to kayak… They are all on my radar. Not for me, but for other women I may meet. *I jokingly offered to write the artist a "highly recommended" addition to his Match.com profile and **did** give him some minor edits.*

We singles are quick to tell one another about store sales, happy hours and reasonably priced handymen, I think we need to be more generous and assertive in sharing people as well. Now obviously, it would be wildly uncomfortable to send your recent three-month fling to a best friend, but with time and space, even some of your more intimate connections might be worthy of passing along. The meet-and-greets that didn't click? For me, that's an obvious "Why not?"

If it won't really hurt you, and it might help them… Think about it. You could be the avenue to happy beginnings for two other people! Dating a guy you aren't into is philanthropy. Passing him on to someone who will truly appreciate him—altruism. Aim to be an altruist.

Building Your Personal Network

So how do you meet all these wonderful new friends? Great question. As I said earlier, I had no idea how to make friends as a newly divorced single. When I had young children, it was easy—my kids created opportunities for me at their schools and playgrounds. With older kids and no husband, it was all up to me—and quite intimidating.

You are going to have to push yourself. It may feel uncomfortable the first time or two (or three), but keep in mind that this will undoubtedly change your life in a significantly positive way.

Start with your neighborhood and work colleagues. Those are easy and obvious. Be open to other women at the gym and any of your other regular hangouts. And then it's time to start Googling the networking options in your city.

Use search terms such as "networking," "social networking," "business networking" and "singles events." Most towns have a number of professional organizations. Some of these will be geared to specific ages, so fine-tune your search by Googling "average ages" (or shoot the leader an inquiry on the group's demographics) to get an idea of the general tenor of various groups. Philanthropic and sports related groups are great choices because they provide an alternate focus, removing some of that first-day-of-school pressure.

Check out "MeetUps" in your area. Chances are you will find weekly groups meeting to kayak, dance, watch movies, critique books and hike, cycle or drink wine. You will generally find singles similarly intent on growing their lives and connections. You will most likely find some new friends.

My city has GETDOT, a philanthropic business/social networking group with monthly events. Low-key gatherings allow for friendships to develop naturally and over time. Philanthropic and charity organizations are always looking for help, and many people make valuable new connections by volunteering for specific annual events.

I also am a regular attendee at several business networking events. These have a two-fold purpose: I make business connections but also find the occasional new friend as well. Not all of them will bloom, but that's no judgment on me.

Remember, others' behaviors are most often not about you at all!

My friend Danielle and I met at the gym, through her ex-husband Randy. Our friendship is the best thing that came out of their roller coaster relationship. Adrianne and I met in a high school track meet bathroom where I'd fled to find temporary warmth. Anna, Sandra and I met at a women-only networking dinner.

Be ready. New friends are everywhere and can make your life fun again, exposing you to new activities and their circles of additional potential friends.

Effective Strategies for Growth

1) Friends First. Friend time goes on the calendar right after time scheduled for my kids and work. I do at least one happy hour/dinner evening a week with a friend or friends, at least one coffee or lunch and one larger networking event—and my gym and park visits almost always include a friend. Alone time goes on the calendar next. As my children grow more independent, solitary moments aren't as elusive as they once were. While I am fully open to dating, I don't have big calendar gaps that are "lacking a relationship."

2) Be a Sharer. I introduce my friends to one another. Many of us have made a decision to be as inclusive as possible— *let no woman (or man) sit home alone!* Not to say we don't schedule one-on-one time with one another as well, but it's very important to us to help others build their own networks and get similarly connected.

3) Actively Search. I look for versions of my past self at the gym, the grocery and networking events and try to hook them up with other people. Divorced and lonely women in waiting rooms, new-to-town students and employees, grocery clerks, soccer moms, singles who have never married… Sometimes I'm just a launcher, pointing them towards the right trail; other times I find a new friend for myself.

4) Choose the Lifestyle. I have made business/social-networking events a priority. Strategically integrating these opportunities into my life has paid off in significant ways. Instead of tying knots to new connections, I aim to weave my contacts together—creating a tapestry of those connections rather than loosely twined strings of macramé business card holders.

5) Effective Follow Up. Many networking events are the adult version of Trick-or-Treat night. Would-be connectors walk out of a breakfast or happy hour with a fistful of business cards, and the general impression that they've made some great new contacts. Many miss this very important next step—the Follow Up—out of the mistaken assumption that the other people will do all the work. *"We had such a great conversation, but I hate to bother him/her. She/He said, 'let's get together/let's stay in touch,' so, I'll just wait on an email or phone call."*

The problem is: People are far too busy and many of our best intentions never launch—*Remember it's not always about you. It's often **their** deadlines, distractions and difficulties that get in the way.*

So make it a point to do the following within 24 hours of the event: 1) Spread out those business "playing" cards and pick out your best hand of ongoing connections. 2) Send out quick emails or LinkedIn connection requests, noting the event and what you discussed—*"Hi Grant. Best wishes on the upcoming product launch—let's schedule that coffee! I could meet with you (fill in a couple of specific options) if that works on your side,"* or *"Hey Linda. It was great chatting with you at yesterday's breakfast! There's a great happy hour networking event next Thursday. Let me know if you're interested."*

A business card is *not* a connection. A Facebook, LinkedIn

or Twitter link is getting closer, but your goal is to create real face-to-face relationships with real human beings. You are not being pushy. Someone has to initiate, and you are offering something very valuable—connection. Whether business or social, create the contact, make it real and then allow it to grow organically. You have to give people calendar space to turn them into true connections. And some of these business or social connections may grow into friendships, or even possibly, relationships—or be conduits to a future relationship with a friend of your new friend.

Go ahead and get dizzy on the possibilities. Even if the most you get are some valuable business allies and a couple of new friends— Wow! That's already more than you had, isn't it?

6) Create and Cherish Your Inner Circle. I regularly reach out to friends via phone calls and email. Our lives are frenetic at times. We travel. We get slammed at work. Our kids' schedules drive our own at times. But none of us should ever land in a news story that leads with "She kind of kept to herself. We just noticed that mail was piling up…" Some of us have little in the way of family, so we have done some pruning and grafting: We call one another "grafted sisters" because we've added one another to our family trees. These are my "Cabernet Coaches," my Tribunal of Friends. With honesty, kindness and encouragement, we hold one another accountable to stated principals and decisions. If one of us loses the way, or simply misses a turn, another one of us will be nearby, map in hand.

CHAPTER ELEVEN

❧

PERSONALIZE YOUR PLAN

ONE OF OUR BIGGEST HURDLES can be the realization that not everyone will like us. Hopefully, we don't give them obvious reasons to dislike us—but men (and women) can have non-reasons (jealousies, prejudices, unresolved hurts) that may affect their opinion of you. Do the *Shoulder Shrug*. This can't impact who you are. That should be solid—growing and evolving—but at its core, structurally sound.

Our long drawn out apologies are often futile attempts at people pleasing. "I'm sorry" should be enough for minor missteps. When "I'm sorry" isn't big enough to bridge a small misunderstanding? It's not about you. Shoulder shrug. When you get that feeling it's time to stop talking—you're right. Stop. And then when you feel embarrassed for talking too long? Shoulder shrug. Life's too short, you aren't his garbage man and maybe he needs to take care of his own stuff.

Be yourself without apology—if you truly value yourself and others, none should be necessary. Our uniqueness defines us, and is often the reason a "good guy" may turn out to be an

"Almost" instead of a "right fit." That's as it should be. Finding that unique person who will enhance your life—just as you will enrich his—shouldn't be a simple endeavor. We may have been shortsighted starter women in our 20s, but by our 40s and beyond we've developed into rich complex women with high-end perspectives, experiences and goals.

This is the part of your life where you get to be a better version of one of the cool kids. So enjoy it and make up for those times you blew it—by ignoring, criticizing or trying to start your own orbit system with yourself as head planet—by applying grownup behaviors to all areas of your life. Even dating.

Define the Ground Rules

If you've landed beyond "needy"—*and we all pit stop there at some point on the journey*—if you've accepted and forgiven the failures of yourselves and others and come to terms with "unfair," you're ready to Date Like a Grownup. And the first thing you will need to do is define how that standard will apply in your own life.

You and I are different—*you're one of those organized, "let's have the soccer team families over for dinner" women, aren't you? That's OK. I'll get over it.* Our ethics and standards will accordingly differ, but here are some basic value choices most of us can agree on:

Dating Ethic Choices

1) Kindness: Dating with kindness includes direct communication even when it's hard to say "no." Kindness will not allow you to disappear from an interested man without explanation and it will not permit you to simply ignore online emails from men you aren't interested in. It leaves no room for taking advantage of a man's willingness to buy you dinner if you are fully aware that you want nothing more than a meal. Aim not to become another bad date anecdote.

2) Respectfulness: You will respect yourself and you will respect the men you date—or you will not date them. Self-respect means no chasing after red herrings or offering your body in hopes of securing his heart. Respect for your date means giving him an honest chance, appreciating that his feelings matter too and accepting his differences. You don't have to make him an ongoing part of your life, but you will at least accept him as a valuable human being.

3) Mindfulness: Grownups make choices. They don't get drunk and "accidentally" sleep with the man they've been lusting after. They get to know him over time. They don't lead other men on while they're trying to decide. They make "yes" and "no" decisions. They engage in the present conversation—their eyes don't flit around the room looking for an upgrade. If they decide "no thank you," they excuse themselves and leave without faking an "emergency."

4) Authenticity: Authentic people don't fake anything. They are kind, but they don't spew polite half-truths. They are essentially the same person whether meeting with a teacher, paying the cash register clerk or at happy hour with their girlfriends. They may laugh a little more at the latter and toss off a sex joke that would never fly in a classroom—but that's just discretion at work.

5) Integrity: Your actions match your words and your thoughts. You don't say, "That sounds fun!" when you're thinking, "I'd rather hose out the garage than try this again." You aren't indefinitely "busy." He is a fine person, but you just aren't interested. *"But I'd love to keep in touch. I keep thinking you might really enjoy getting to know this one really great friend of* *mine.*" Grownups do not date married men, because then they would have to lead a double life. They clean up old messes before beginning new relationships.

6) Appreciation: Grownups are appreciative of their life as a whole and of the individuals who pass though it specifically. Whether long-term friends or meet-and-greet dates, they are thankful for opportunities and experiences, aiming to learn from them. They have no set expectations regarding what they will learn.

Setting Your Personal Standards

Lonely stretches of time can lead to reckless choices. Avoid these by filling in the answers ahead of time. Who will you date? Who will you not date? Where will you meet? How soon will you share your personal information?

1) Choose Your Cabernet Coaches. Pick these women and men carefully. They are your inner circle and privy to many of your personal decisions. Maintain regular contact and consider their perspectives. These men and women represent an important foundational element in your life. Aim to be the same for them, investing in their lives as well.

2) Identify Your Dating Pool. Are you ready to post an online dating profile? Will you include neighbors, gym members, office colleagues and fellow parents in your pool of potential attachments? There's no "yes" or "no" on this one—just degrees of potential awkwardness. Generally, it's better to date one of the latter only if you already know them pretty well. No "cold calls," date only the pre-qualified individuals within your immediate circles.

3) Keep it Safe. What's an acceptable place for a first meeting with a blind date or online contact? Aim for public spaces. No parks and no areas of town you aren't fully familiar with. Coffee shops, restaurants, even grocery stores… Be creative, but keep it safe.

4) Sharing Personal Contact Information. When will you allow a man to pick you up from your residence? Giving a stranger your last name, address and employment information is a potential risk. Common friends and a LinkedIn presence can help build your comfort level, but ultimately trust your gut. And always try to inform a friend or adult family member of your plans.

5) Keep it Short. Make any first meeting of an online contact or blind date a meet-and-greet rather than an actual date. Give yourself—and him—the appropriate wiggle room to exit as needed. Don't take it personally if he skedaddles after a single cup of coffee. Be polite if *you* feel the need to make an early exit.

6) Remember Your Mission. Find out who he is too. First meetings should be a two-way conversation. If you aren't curious about him and his life—move on. If you *never* ask questions, do a self-check to see if you have allowed yourself to be self-centered or are too focused on "winning" a guy, rather than discovering who he is and how he might fit your life.

7) Refrain From Comparisons. Make yes or no decisions. Evaluate the potential for a relationship with the guy in front of you in the present moment. Try to avoid comparison-shopping.

8) Pace Yourself. Space it out. Whether meeting a series of men from an online site or getting to know one particular guy, don't make it a marathon experience. Give yourself space to think and continue living the rest of your life.

9) Facilitate Cooperation. How will you handle schedule change requests with your ex? It will be in your own best interest to cultivate a civil relationship with your former spouse. Besides the obvious benefit of more effective joint parenting, nurturing a healthier version of your doomed marital relationship will make growing any new relationship a lot easier. But decide how *much* you are willing to share in advance. "I have a conflict with a weekend next month" versus "Can you watch the kids that weekend so Ron and I can go camping?" Generally, less is better when it comes to spilling romantic details to an ex, but if you're able to actively enable one another's rebuilding process, it's almost always a "win/win." Express your willingness to be flexible on scheduling, and prove it by going first. In the beginning, it's smart to be specific, "Why don't we swap the Monday you need free for the following Thursday?" Email these kinds of schedule changes to maintain a clearly traceable record. Your ex is bitter? Then try again later. Never close that door.

10) Sexual Boundaries. I encourage you to make physical intimacy a decision, rather than an impulse. At the least, set a time frame and general conditions. And don't make it "when he says 'I love you.'" Some guys will say anything to get everything. And how will you handle the matter of sexual histories and potential STDs? This is another vitally important reason for getting to know someone very well before venturing into physical intimacy.

11) Introductions. When will you introduce a potential "Right Guy" to friends and family? Set a loose sort of timeframe for yourself. If introduction opportunities come and go a few times, this may be a signal that the "Right Guy" is really an "Almost Guy."

12) Including Children. When is the "right time" to introduce children? What will you need to see in a guy to allow him across this important boundary and what length of time will establish these behaviors and attitudes as consistent, and therefore, most likely to be authentic? This is a critical choice.

More single parents err with a "too early" introduction than by waiting too long.

The "Don'ts"

1) Don't lie. Don't be untruthful about your lifestyle, your career goals, your past or your current status. Don't lie about your intentions or feelings. If you don't know how you feel, say so.

2) Don't spill too much too soon. Getting to know a potential love interest should take a little time. Yes, it's thrilling to want to talk all night, but don't reveal your whole history on the first date.

3) Don't allow a man to spend money and time on you if you aren't attracted to him. No gifts; no big dinners; no maintenance jobs around your house. Don't be a "user."

Caveat: If a platonic guy friend offers to help you with a house project, say, "Yes, thank you" and cook him dinner—or help him with something in return (maybe fix him up with that HR gal you met last week?). Friends help friends.

4) Don't be a disappearing friend. Be consistent with your friends, your families and your activities. Don't jump tracks to follow the path of a guy you think you might want to date.

Send Clear Messages

Most of us are excessively uncomfortable with even the possibility of confrontation. Maybe we've never learned effective navigation via direct dialogue or it could be a residual desire to be "liked" that gets in the way of being honest, but one of the biggest needs for dating adults is straightforward communication.

I used to be absolutely horrible at this. *"I don't want to hurt his feelings…"* The truth is I didn't want to witness his feelings getting hurt and deal with the aftermath. A courteous explanation was beyond my capabilities, so instead, I whined about the difficulty of telling someone what they didn't want to hear.

Men and women alike say nothing and hope that the other will "get the message." They feign interest when they're yawning on the inside. Singles say "maybe" when they really mean "no." This lame approach to delivering "bad news" creates bigger messes in the end. It stretches stress beyond a five-minute phone call into five days of subterfuge.

Honesty really is the best policy. It saves time and dignity.

Need words? I've helped a lot of my friends compose messages and plan conversations. Feel free to use these field-tested *"Useable and Effective Responses."*

From the Field: *"Useable and Effective Responses"*

Worried about finding the right words? Below I've outlined various scenarios with suggestions for verbal or written navigation.

That Guy at the Gym/Grocery/Bookstore

"Thanks, but I'm not looking to date right now"—*and you aren't at that moment in time when there's a sale on sweet potatoes.*

Your Online Email "No Thank You" Response

"Thanks so much for the email, but" a) "I'm looking for someone closer to my own zip code," b) "I couldn't be comfortable with our age difference" or c) "I'm looking for someone who shares more of my primary interests."

If you'd like to give his wings some lift, open with "You seem like a great guy for the right woman, but…"

If they make a rude sexual comment, your silence (and blocking his profile) is response enough.

A Meet-and-Greet "One and Done"

If he asks about getting together again: "Thanks for taking the time to meet me. I don't really see this developing into the kind of relationship I think we each deserve, but I wish you the very best."

If you think he'd make a great friend or date for a friend: "While I don't see the two of us developing more than a friendship, I really value my friendships and would love to keep in touch. Maybe I can introduce you to some of my other single friends. You never know!" Or you could add, "I'm always looking for friends who enjoy (fill in the activity)."

If he doesn't ask for another date, he may simply be pacing himself. Regardless, text a thank you for the drink and then a variation of one of the above, shortened for texting: "Nice chatting with you. Don't think we click in the ways necessary for dating, but I'd love to introduce you to some of my friends."

If the date was excruciating: "Thanks for the drink. Don't think we click in the right ways for dating, but I hope you find somebody special."

Your "First Date/Last Date" Response

These can be very similarly worded, but these guys deserve a phone call rather than a text message. Be classy and do a quick phone call towards the end of the workday—not right before their 9am meeting. Always ask if it's a good moment to talk before you launch into your "no thank you."

"I've really enjoyed getting to know you a little better, but I can tell this won't go the distance we're both aiming for. Many thanks for last night. And I'd love to keep in touch if you're willing. I have some great friends!"

Of course, if he tried to lay the groundwork for date two at the end of date one, you already covered it kindly and honestly on the spot, right?

Responding to "But I Like You! We Could Have Something Special!"

OK. He's pulling out the heavy artillery and is revealing some unattractive neediness. A guy may be highly attracted to you, but the absence of immediately visible red flags does not make you a perfect woman. *Did he not see you fumble that meatball and kick it under the table?!* These are the Cling Wrap guys.

Here's your response: "You seem like a great guy who's ready for a real relationship. You deserve someone who can grow those feelings with you. I just can't see that happening with me, and anything less than that wouldn't be fair to either of us. I do wish you the very best."

Letting Down an "Almost" Guy

Whether this reached intimate stages or not, you've spent some time with this man. No phone breakups. He deserves a face-to-face conversation, so that he can cut the tie and move on with his life. Meeting in a public place is easier—you'll have the opportunity to make an exit. But if you think he will feel emotional, choose carefully. Consider a park or parking lot with a little privacy.

Find your bullet points first: a) You like him. b) It just isn't working for you. c) You value the time spent together. d) He deserves more than you will be able to give him emotionally.

If he asks what he did or for more time or for anything you're unwilling to give, simply say, "I'm sorry. This just isn't going to grow into the relationship we each deserve."

Now if he did something really stupid or offensive, you can skip the "I like you" part, but be civil. He probably knows that passing out at your sister's didn't enchant any of your family. Just say that you're sorry, but that it simply isn't going to work out—and that your sister wants the lampshade back.

Saying Goodbye to a Long-Term Love

Breaking off a long-term relationship that has fallen into the "heavy lifting" zone mentioned in Chapter Nine is always going to be hard no matter who initiates the breakup process.

You have a favorite restaurant and song, a weekend routine and have discussed a future together. You know he bobs his head when he brushes his teeth. He knows you like extra wasabi with your sushi, and that you won't eat it without chopsticks.

You may be ambivalent. The last few months have been hard, but are your challenges truly insurmountable? Is he a good guy but not the right guy? Or could he be the right guy dealing with a difficult life circumstance? I can't give you a clear answer on this kind of decision, but I'll say this:

If you've invested time in a relationship, you'll want to invest a few more days into determining your next steps. Couples counseling is always a valid option in making this, often, monumental decision.

Having been a marriage "quitter," I'm more likely to give extra leeway to potential solutions. But sometimes, the best words will be "thank you" and "good-bye."

No, you may never know the ending to his life story—you'll have to "unfriend" and "disconnect" on this one—and that might be excruciatingly difficult, but you aren't his mom or his teacher. You are an "ex." Hopefully, you added to his life experience, but your time with him is over.

There is no single "good-bye" response for a "Could Have Been." Some of the language above may apply for the disengagement period, but chances are that this will take a month or more as the "good-bye" moves from possible to probable to official.

Find your friends and get busy. Don't yank him back after you've let him go. But don't be a bridge burner either. It's better to break an inanimate object (*glassware, china or a biodegradable egg…*) than a heart and a potential pathway for a better time in the future. You will never regret kindness. Even if he doesn't have the capacity for it, you will have no regrets for choosing grownup behavior here.

At the least, you'll know that you ended well, and that counts.

CHAPTER TWELVE

DATE LIKE A GROWNUP

From the Field: *"If We'd Had Happy Hour in High School..."*

I scanned the table, relaxed, with my happy hour cabernet in hand and an appetizer on the way. One of my sisters, recently separated, was laughing with a now mutual friend of mine. Adrianne, Marnie, Barb and Brenda were there. Kind of an eclectic group really...

My once-estranged sister Stephanie and I were in the beginning stages of building our first real relationship with one another. We'd each traveled through hell, but on separate trails. Now, we were learning to share our journeys.

Adrianne, I had met while attempting to warm up in a high school bathroom during a track meet. She looked up with an effervescent smile and said, "We're connected on LinkedIn!" She became one of my dearest friends and cheerleaders; hauled me to medical appointments and even dress shopping when I was in a leg cast and just generally enriched my life.

Marnie, now Adrianne's friend as well, who flirted with the guy I was dancing with the night we met—*She didn't know.* She makes me laugh several times a day—*every* day—and has yet to discover how truly special she is...

Barb, an attorney I met through a local networking group. She surprised me the first time we finally got together for a drink. Her quiet somewhat serious demeanor belies a very thoughtful, funny, warmhearted woman I've grown to cherish.

And Brenda, my old high school friend. We had virtually reconnected via Facebook, but we took it to the next level and redeveloped a face-to-face, heart-to-heart friendship that far exceeds what we dabbled with on our way to Geometry class.

The faces change, but Wednesday happy hours are semi-sacred. We'll occasionally let a guy in, especially if I think he might click with a friend, but it's a "ladies first" night for me. While I try to connect with my women friends one-on-one, this is the regular gathering when all else fails. Janis is often there, another high school friend and total sports nut, whose still waters run deeper than I'd ever guessed. And Kayron, Barb's roommate and now also my friend, who has many of the same scars I do, but who has also mustered the muscle to move beyond them to create a better life.

Marnie once teased me about disappearing after I met John (of Chapter Three) in August of 2013 (*Yep, it really happened! I finally met the man I wanted to kiss!*), and I didn't respond well. "Never! I'll never be one of those disappearing women. You're part of my life. Remember? I grafted you onto my family tree as a sister!"

And that's the simple truth. My friends lost no value to me when I met a man. They're part of this life I love. John has met many of them and knows how much they mean to me. Frankly, if John and I *only* hung out with one another, even my super smart, sweet guy would get boring. Life is bigger than the two of us, alone or together.

In addition to the women mentioned above, Lilly, Dawn, Eileen, my cousins Laura and Holly, my Aunt Sue and sisters Stephanie, Suzanne and Kathleen are foundational to the life I've built. Some women friends have been "for a season," which is why I always advise my daughter to "make many," but most have remained woven into my life, and pulling them loose would completely destroy the fabric of it.

Brenda and I had the fun task of shooting the cover for this book. Ironically, she used to play piano for me in high school while I sang, and now, she was taking my photo as I mugged for the camera on a warm October afternoon.

We wandered Old Worthington, much as we had on high school lunch breaks, but with a comfortable confidence that we lacked as ninth graders.

"Laura and I hated that you would *never* talk about sex!" Brenda told me.

"That's because I knew nothing real *about* it! I was probably embarrassed! And it was such a taboo subject with my mom and..."

Brenda nodded. We'd already shared the missing back-stories, safely hidden in our cautiously veneered youth. "Yeah. I always thought you were Miss Perfect, and I remember Laura telling me it wasn't all as it seemed."

"And you seemed sooo mature..."

Brenda laughed. "Far from it."

"We showed what we thought people wanted and saw what we wanted to see. Did you know that Laura and I met in the bathroom between classes in eighth grade—trying to cover up our zits?"

Brenda laughed again. "Nope. Hadn't heard that one. Now turn a little. Can you tip your head that way? Yes! That's great. Perfect!" Snap. Snap. Snap. Snap.

Eventually, we wandered to The Worthington Inn, and although Sunday brunch was over, we talked our way into glasses of cabernet on the front porch. For photographic purposes, we said. I haven't seen those shots yet, but Brenda tells me they turned out to be the best ones.

I DON'T REMEMBER when the phrase first popped in my head, but it quickly became a regular—*unlike the voice that's supposed to remind me where I parked.*

A friend would offer to do a text rescue as I headed out to a questionable meet-and-greet: *"I'll text an emergency. Use it if you need it."*

"No thanks. I'm going to date like a grownup this time."

Or I remember a neighbor—yeah, one of **them**—commenting on unwanted Match.com emails: *"I just delete 'em."*

"I can't do that! I'm trying to date like a grownup this time!"

"Date like a grownup." What did that really mean?

At first, it was simple elimination: No "hide in the bathroom" behavior, no "Oops, I have to get off the phone" disconnects and no pretensions. I wanted to be a "positive," regardless of ultimate outcome. I wanted to be me—that seemed a lot easier than trying to fit someone else's standard for a woman. Maybe if I picked the right guy, the "right fit" for my personality—that would be possible?

It was a promising start. I went online and met a lot of nice guys. They were all so damned nice. They all deserved a kind-hearted, genuine woman. Brain overload. I couldn't date them all.

From there I grew selective. During high school and college—the first time around—my mantra had been "Does he like me?" I shifted now to "Do I like him? Could he enhance my life?" This was a significant change. Instead of merely looking confident—*apparently mild frozen panic plays as "poised" in high school*—I began *feeling* confident. No, I had only vague ideas of how to fertilize my lawn and trap a mouse, but I began solving my own problems and feeling more "substantial" as a person.

Success made me greedy for more. I traveled solo, took my kids kayaking and on wild hiking adventures up and down mountains and through slot canyons—and managed to strand us on a Puerto Rican island (temporarily). I biked, hiked and ran to remote areas with no backup but my own wits and a useless cell phone. I made new friends. Began writing for real. I took chances and risked failures.

I guess I became more of a grownup myself.

Still, I found myself selecting from options instead of selecting "the guy." I was "shopping" and determined to make a purchase. When a holiday or new season approached, I found myself wondering if I'd be spending it with someone... If I'd be in a relationship by "then."

Some pivotal moments led to a pivotal perspective change.

The first happened during a solo trip to Mexico. My kids were vacationing with their dad, and rather than mope alone, I'd attacked the empty space by venturing to Nuevo Vallarta. "Solo" was hard. But ultimately, it was exceptionally meaningful, allowing me to see glimpses of the stronger woman I would one day grow to be. Towards the end of my week, after an afternoon spent with new friends exploring the rocky crags and teeming waters around the Marietas Islands, I finally hit "pause."

My week had been jammed with long runs along the beach, zip lining in the nearby jungle and on-foot solo explorations of nearby cities. I'd kept busy, hunkering down in my room to write during my solo evenings, ignoring the strains of lively music that tugged my hopes in directions my feet longed to follow.

But as the teak-hulled sailboat drew away from the Marietas' cliffs teaming with frigates and blue-footed booby birds while the sun blazed on a sparkling sea and the crisp white sails were raised, I experienced what I like to call a "perfect moment." What was unusual about this one was to experience that surge of joy all by myself, without children or close friends or a man. What a revelation: that a tree could fall within its forest and that my ear alone could be enough to hear and mark its sound. Bliss could wrap its arms around me, just me. It didn't have to be a group hug.

Another shift occurred when I underwent my post-traumatic stress therapy. Barriers fell, and I could finally see the sky unencumbered by branches of my past blocking the way. I began to recognize my own possibilities rather than to feel dependent upon fitting into the potentials of others. I quit looking for men I could "help" to be their best and focused instead on becoming my own best self.

Surprisingly, even with all the "my's" and "I's" sprinkled into that last paragraph, it became *less* about me than it had ever been. I (mostly) lost that niggling need for affirmation and grew more concerned with affirming others still settled into the rut I'd lived in. Many of us one-time married moms are used to hooking our wagons to the lives of others. Driving our own lives is a new concept—frightening at times, but ultimately, an empowering, exhilarating experience!

I focused on building friendships—deeply valued connections with both men and women, rather than searching for my next relationship. In the past, it was easier for me to do a solo thirty miles on my bike than to reach out to make plans for next Wednesday night. Connecting became my priority.

Which brought about my third perspective changer...

A bad sprain in August of 2010 eventually led me back to a surgeon's office—my cumulative damage was severe enough that the doctor recommended an ankle fusion, devastating news to an active woman like myself. Months of research led me to a better option, but I still faced eight weeks on crutches with no driving allowed.

I was afraid. A single, self-employed mom? How would I do this alone? I'd been a married woman with in-home help the last time I'd faced such a challenge.

But I discovered I wasn't alone at all. Single—yes. But with a network of friends now that was more than up for the task of getting me through my challenge. As I mentioned in Chapter Ten, they toted me everywhere I needed or wanted to go. I was "single" but surrounded by love in a way I hadn't experienced before.

Dating like a grownup means respecting myself enough not to make finding a relationship a disproportionate priority. It means respecting the men I choose to date by ending relationships that don't work and by valuing men as people first and a possible "forever guy" second. It means making plans for next weekend, next month and next summer and not waiting to see if someone will be there to experience it with me. It means grasping my life with both hands, being ready to share it, but appreciating it so much that I will never release that grip.

I like to imagine a golden crescent of a beach, waves lapping softly across the packed sand of the shoreline. An expanse of soft white sand spreads from there on toward a rise of dunes. The water is warm, the sun burns hot and the breeze is cool. We can approach this scene with a metal detector in hand, intent on searching out a particular treasure or we can swim, surf, run, build sand castles, play beach volleyball…

At the end of the day—or a life—the metal detector may signal a valuable discovery buried deep beneath the sand. Or not. Upon digging, the "treasure" may be a rusted anchor or broken chain. On the other hand, if we explore all the opportunities of the beach, we will reach the end of the day—or life—grateful for the experiences enjoyed and fulfilled. And it is entirely possible that we'll kick up a treasure worth keeping while diving for the ball on that beach.

Even grownups like beach volleyball.

NOTES

<u>1</u> "If she's amazing, she won't be easy. If she's easy, she won't be amazing. If she's worth it, you won't give up. If you give up, you're not worthy… Truth is, everybody is going to hurt you; you just gotta find the ones worth suffering for. "—commonly attributed to Bob Marley

<u>2</u> To seek counseling is an act of courage. Deciding to take a closer look at potential glitches in your own thought patterns is a confident choice to grab hold of your own steering wheel. Those that categorically dismiss the therapy option—"I don't need help"—are often secretly afraid of what they might discover. Finding distractions is easier and definitely more popular, but ultimately, a waste of time and your potential. You might not need "help," but why not give yourself every opportunity for success? If you have been through a divorce—or never been able to sustain a long-term relationship—please make this investment in yourself. *Do it for your own children, so that you can model "healthy"—I promise it will look good on you.* And if alcoholism or drug abuse of any kind has tainted your life

or the lives of your ex, your kids or any close family member, I have friends who would urge you to try Al-Anon or Alcoholics Anonymous—to open doors far wider and more positively than you could ever imagine.

ACKNOWLEDGEMENTS

Here's to *Love*... This book grew out of love and regard for my single friends, but is ultimately the product of so much love returned. My deepest thanks to all who shared their personal stories—thus allowing others the possibility of learning from their mistakes and heartbreaks.

"Thanks" also to my patient and oh-so-helpful readers: Bob Brancato, John Damschroder, Laura Frongillo, Michael Gould, Dennis Hetzel, Barb Letcher, Monda Sue Prior and Mark Wyckoff—tough critic but true friend. Your attention to detail blanketed in warm encouragement was critical to the success (and punctuation) in this book. Deep gratitude and a toast to my Cabernet Coaches, both married and single: Adrianne Benson, Dawn Bryant Mather, Kayron Charlesworth, Lilly Dixon, Janis Frankenburg, Brenda Butler Kerns, Barb Letcher, Marnie Medlock and Eileen Shihab. We share freely, speak the truth, affirm one another's considerable abilities and meet for happy hours and heart-to-hearts. May it always be so...

To my three children, Zak, Hannah and Matt: Your support means more than you could possibly know. Thanks for loving me as I am, enthusiastic and occasionally distracted by inspiration, and for accompanying me on so many memorable adventures. I love you dearly, deeply and completely. May the three of you flourish where your parents faltered; choose well and ultimately share your dreams with a life-long love. And to their cousins, my cherished nieces and nephews: "Family" is given; connection is a choice. Protect and fortify those bonds between you. Cousins and siblings can be your best lifelong friends. My parents, gone but never forgotten: Thank you for giving the best you had to give. *With fond memories of my Dad who was my first "fan", and inspired me to, eventually, believe in my own possibilities.* To my sisters, Stephanie Marxen, Suzanne Van Schaik and Kathleen Hadder: Who knew we'd get do-overs? Dibs on the window seat, but here's to the ride... To my Massachusetts family, Monda Sue Prior, Laura Frongillo, Holly LeBart and Spencer Laemmele: You've filled the gaps with love and friendship and cemented your places in my heart.

And thank you, John Damschroder. You found my heart and trusted me with your own. Our adventures have only just begun. *Smile.*

ABOUT THE AUTHOR

A nationally published writer, columnist and author as well as a voiceover and video talent/producer, Heather's focus is on creative communication and human connection. Projects range from books, articles and a national advice column to travel, eLearning and corporate videos. Death? Divorce? Dating? Done, done and done. Turning challenges into opportunities for achievement enabled this divorced single mom to effect positive transformation and even find value in life's darkest places. Helping others to tap into their talents and "launch" is now a primary passion, and Heather's public speaking and radio/TV interview topics include life launching; divorce, dating and relationships; healthcare patient responsibility and work/family issues. She is active in numerous networking organizations and serves on the board of GETDOT, a group dedicated to facilitating connection while raising money for local children's charities. Books include

"Pickup in Aisle Twelve," and "Stuffing Sandwiches Down My Shirt: Strategies & Inspiration for Crutch Users."

Passionately curious, Heather is both a dedicated traveler and lifelong learner. She resides in Central Ohio with her children and a wayward chocolate lab, is slightly addicted to the outdoors and would never let her passport expire. She considers humor to be her best accessory.

Links to books and audio/video clips can be found at her website: http://www.HeatherDugan.com. She enjoys connecting with readers via social media and email.

www.DateLikeAGrownup.net
www.CabernetCoaches.com

ALSO BY HEATHER DUGAN

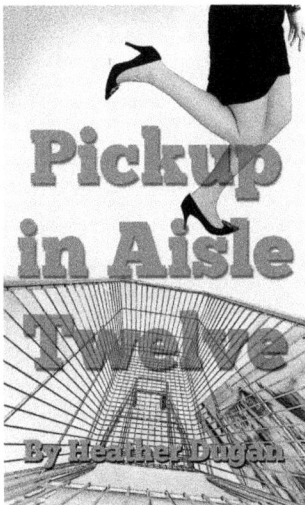

Pickup in Aisle Twelve After a would-be suitor tails her to a grocery store checkout, Angie Wharton confronts the grim realities of her post-divorce dating options. Niggling guilt, a fickle resolve and easy access to her sister's dinner table have kept her on the sidelines, but her brother-in-law's patience—and supplies of cabernet are running low.

Pressed into posting an online dating profile, Angie decides to take the offense before love passes her by. But navigating this virtual world of blurred photos and lonely hearts will require her to create both a roadmap and a new understanding of herself.

Lipstick? Check. Eye contact? More or less. Awkward moments? Uh huh. Love…?

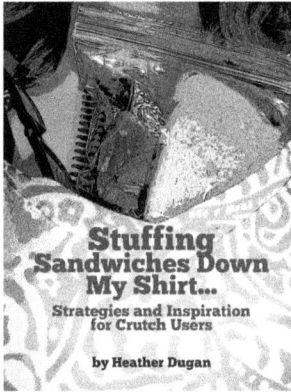

Stuffing Sandwiches Down My Shirt: Strategies and Inspiration for Crutch Users An upbeat approach to one-footed living, this book delivers practical ideas for maximizing the temporary challenges associated with a casted leg and crutch use. The author, a single mom of three, found humor to be critical in making her post-op recovery time a fulfilling and, surprisingly, fun experience. Gym workouts, grocery shopping and even happy hours still happened—she deemed her cast to be "better than a puppy" in facilitating human connection.

www.ingramcontent.com/pod-product-compliance
Lightning Source LLC
Chambersburg PA
CBHW060034030426
42334CB00019B/2318